the ultimate
Southern Living
CHRISTMAS
BOOK

the ultimate
Southern Living
CHRISTMAS
BOOK

compiled and edited by
Rebecca Brennan and Allison Long Lowery

©2003 by Oxmoor House, Inc.
Book Division of Southern Progress Corporation
P.O. Box 2463, Birmingham, Alabama 35201

Southern Living® is a federally registered trademark belonging to Southern Living, Inc.

ISBN: 0-8487-2729-0
Printed in the United States of America
First Printing 2003

Southern Living®
Contributing Editors: Derick Belden, Stephen P. Bender, Cynthia Ann Briscoe, Gene B. Bussell, Lynnmarie P. Cook, Susan Dosier, Donna Florio, Melanie Grant, Eleanor Griffin, Julia Hamilton, Andria Scott Hurst, Scott Jones, Robert C. Martin, Susan Hawthorne Nash, Kate Nicholson, Ellen Ruoff Riley, Charles Thigpen, Joy E. Zacharia
Test Kitchens Director: Lyda H. Jones
Recipe Development Director: Mary Allen Perry
Test Kitchens Staff: Rebecca Kracke Gordon, Vanessa A. McNeil, James Schend, Angela Sellers, Vie Warshaw
Contributing Photographers: Jean M. Allsopp, Ralph Anderson, Van Chaplin, Tina Cornett, William Dickey, Laurey W. Glenn, John O'Hagan, Charles Walton IV
Contributing Photo Stylists: Cindy Manning Barr, Buffy Hargett, Lisa M. Powell
Photo Researchers: Ginny P. Allen, Laurl Self, Lisa Trial

Oxmoor House, Inc.
Editor-in-Chief: Nancy Fitzpatrick Wyatt
Executive Editor: Susan Carlisle Payne
Art Director: Cynthia Rose Cooper
Copy Chief: Catherine Ritter Scholl

The Ultimate Southern Living® Christmas Book
Editor: Rebecca Brennan
Foods Editor: Allison Long Lowery
Copy Editors: Donna Baldone, Susan H. Ray
Editorial Assistant: Diane Rose
Senior Designer: Melissa M. Clark
Senior Photographer: Jim Bathie
Photographer: Brit Huckabay
Senior Photo Stylist: Kay E. Clarke
Photo Stylist: Ashley Wyatt
Illustrator: Kelly Davis
Director, Test Kitchens: Elizabeth Tyler Luckett
Assistant Director, Test Kitchens: Julie Christopher
Recipe Editor: Gayle Hays Sadler
Test Kitchens Staff: Kristi Carter, Nicole Faber, Kathleen Royal Phillips, Jan A. Smith, Elise Weis, Kelley Self Wilton
Publishing Systems Administrator: Rick Tucker
Director, Production and Distribution: Phillip Lee
Books Production Manager: Theresa L. Beste
Production Assistant: Faye Porter Bonner

Contributors:
Recipe Indexer: Mary Ann Laurens
Interns: Terri Laschober, Sarah Miller

Front cover (left to right): Ornament Wreath, page 41; Petite Alternatives, page 86; Apricot Pecan Bread, page 171
Back cover (clockwise from top left): Gumdrop Tree, pages 158-159; A Wreath within a Wreath, page 34; Snow Globes, page 223; Add Little Extras, page 237; Dried Citrus Ornament, page 82; Southern Eggnog, page 166; Buttermilk Fudge Squares, page 119

To order additional publications, call 1-800-765-6400.
For more books to enrich your life, visit **oxmoorhouse.com**

contents

greetings

At *Southern Living*, we appreciate traditions, and we know there's no time like Christmas to celebrate time-honored ways to make this magical season of the year the best that it can be. With that in mind, we've collected in this volume our favorite decorating, entertaining, cooking, and gift-giving ideas from over 30 years of Christmas creations from our magazine and books.

As you look through these pages, you'll find ideas for everything that makes planning for the holidays so much fun. And we know how important that is to you. November and December are typically our best-selling newsstand issues for the whole year. Our Holiday Dinners® special section always ranks among the most popular of our magazine features. And in a recent poll of our web site visitors, almost 75% said that they go all out when it comes to planning for Christmas. That's why we know you'll love this book. It includes over 260 decorating ideas for trimming your home, 150 foolproof recipes, plus 9 complete menus. There are over 75 projects for decorating, gifts, and wrappings. And it's all there for you in over 280 beautiful color photographs so you'll be inspired every time you turn the page.

With this book we offer you the best—from the pages of our magazine and from our hearts—for years and years of joyful celebrations.

Becky & Allison

decorating

**doorways • wreaths • garlands
mantels • trees**

12 delightful doorways

OUTDOOR DECORATIONS SHARE THE SPIRIT OF THE SEASON WITH
EVERY PASSERBY. WHETHER YOU FANCY FRUIT OR GREENERY,
THESE FRONT DOORS WILL SHOW YOU NEW WAYS TO SAY WELCOME.

a fresh approach

An evergreen garland intertwined with strings of tiny white lights plays nicely alongside a bright white door. Gold cherubs, accented with lime green and red bows, grace the corners. Large nails tapped into the frame around the door support the garland. The embellishments on the garland and door are held in place with florist wire and picks.

Looking in through the front door, you see that the fanlight and door decorations introduce elements that reappear throughout the home's interior—fresh greenery, ostrich feathers, ribbons, glass ball ornaments, clusters of velvet grapes, and clove-studded lemons. Green apples, a surprise accent for candlesticks on the foyer table, add a burst of color.

set a seasonal tone

Create a holiday theme at your entryway such as the one pictured on the opposite page. Wee carolers and gaily wrapped packages evoke the feeling of a quaint Victorian street corner. Strands of twinkling lights brighten the evergreen trees that flank the doors and the lush garlands that trim the doorway and banisters. Red bells enhance the musical motif.

smooth transition

Repeating the rich colors and materials of this home's exterior decorations in the foyer reinforces the lush decorating scheme. The outdoor's crimson and gold tones are reflected in the vibrant diamond-design ribbon on the indoor banister. Golden pears, grape clusters, berries, and bows are tucked into the greenery and held in place with florist wire. The entrance is made even more grand with the addition of small artificial trees "planted" in urns on the front porch and frosted with tiny white twinkle lights.

simply divine

For astonishing sophistication, add an ordinary rope spray-painted gold to a plain evergreen garland (below). The bold tassels are easy to make; just knot the rope ends and unravel the strands. On the front door, pomegranates and pinecones add color and texture to a mixed greenery wreath. Florist picks and wire hold the fruit and pinecones in place.

naturally grand

An abundantly full mixed greenery garland is the key to the traditional appeal of this doorway (opposite page). Use two garlands (or double a very long garland) or fill in the garland with sprigs of cedar, boxwood, cypress, and pine to give it added volume. Pinecones, red ribbons, and a berry-trimmed wreath on the door complete the classic look.

take a bough

Here are some tips to help you incorporate natural elements into your seasonal decorations.

• A sharp pair of high-quality hand pruners makes cutting greenery easier.

• Use florist wire on a spool to tie greens, ornaments, and other materials together.

• Fresh greenery and lots of simple Southern plants are terrific for both inside and outdoor accents. Their scent lends appeal that artificial ones can't. However, if you prefer to use artificial, tuck branches or sprigs of fresh materials into the arrangement to get the benefit of the wonderful fragrance.

• Soak greenery cuttings in water before using them in decorations, and add a little glycerine or a silicone-like glycerine to the water to prolong their life.

deep south charm

On this front porch, fresh greenery garlands are embellished with two of the South's most traditional plants—lush camellias and delicate Spanish moss. Slipped into water picks, the camellias' light colors accent the greenery. A potted ficus tree on the porch twinkles with white lights. Wide swaths of open-weave, gauzy fabric wind through the garland, and wreaths adorn the double front doors.

You don't have to have ready access to camellias and Spanish moss to achieve this look. Many blooms, such as carnations, are easily found during the holidays to use in place of camellias. For the Spanish moss effect, buy decorative moss in packages from a crafts or floral supply store, and drape it along the length of the garland. This is also a good way to create a fuller look if your garland or wreath seems a little too skimpy.

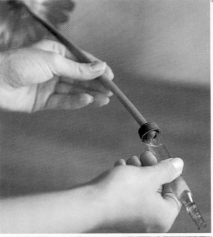

tips for fresh blooms

• Water picks (or vials) are a marvelous invention because they allow you to place cut flowers in some unexpected places, such as wreaths and garlands. Purchase an assortment of sizes from a crafts store, local florist, or grocery store floral department.

• Since cut flowers take up water in amazing quantities, you may want to add them to your greenery only for special occasions. Otherwise, check water picks for moisture levels daily. You may need to refill them frequently.

stockings for the door

Twin wreaths and velvet stockings stuffed with airy white tulips offer guests an out-of-the-ordinary holiday greeting. The entry is framed by a boxwood garland that's draped on three large nails across the top of the door. Trios of limes are secured to the garland with florist picks and florist wire. Bronze-colored twine loops throughout the swag.

You can achieve this look using any type of evergreen garland; however, boxwood typically stays green and doesn't shed. Boxwood generally does well when exposed to Southern winters and stands up fairly well if it's freezing or snowing. A bigger danger is protecting it from windburn on very blustery days or sudden temperature rises on a warm day.

HOW MUCH IS ENOUGH? A good rule of thumb if you'd like to place a garland around your door is to purchase or make about 20 feet of natural garland for each single door. Use extra garland for a mailbox spray.

HOLIDAY HOW-TO

stocking wreath
a twist on the traditional

materials

dried black eyed-peas or beans • 2 large stockings florist picks • 2 (48-ounce) juice cans or lightweight cylinder vases • florist tape • cut flowers or seasonal greenery • greenery clippers • 2 boxwood or greenery wreaths • Spanish moss

1 Place a small amount of peas or beans in toe of stocking as ballast. (Crumpled paper will also work.)

2 Cut two florist picks to form an X-shaped holder to support the container. Place the florist pick holder down into the container; secure it with florist tape.

3 Put the container into the stocking, and hang or secure the stocking to the wreath.

4 Carefully pour water into the container. Do not overfill. Arrange flowers or greenery in each container. For a soft natural look, tuck small strands of Spanish moss into the top of each stocking.

brighten with burlap bows

A simple garland and wreath are complemented by small evergreen trees planted in tall urns and placed on either side of the door. Wide strips of colored burlap tied into bows bring cheer to the evergreen trims. In addition to being a unique creative adornment, burlap is an inexpensive alternative to wide ribbon. Trailing ivy, pansies, and twig balls tied with burlap fill in along the bottom of the trees.

a spiraling sensation

This cedar garland adorned with Granny Smith apples, lemons, and winding ribbon creates quite an impression. Inverted tomato cages placed in planters make quick and easy forms to support the spirals. Use florist picks or thread florist wire through the fruit to attach it to the garland and tomato cages.

23

tall topiaries

Twin topiaries are the star feature at this front door. Full-size Fraser fir trees planted in decorative pots are pruned into topiary shapes.

To create the topiaries, first plant the trees in containers. To shape the trees, using pruning shears, cut the lower branches where they meet the bark. Make the cut as close to the bark as possible, completely pruning the lower part of each tree.

Starting at the top, prune the greenery at a gentle angle, turning the pot as you cut, to ensure evenness. Prune about ¾ inch from the ends of the bottom limbs. Place sheet moss over the soil of the container, and add fresh-cut boughs around the base of the container.

topiary tips

• When using pruning shears, the curve of the shears always should be on the bottom when making a cut.
• To add lights to the topiaries, use small pieces of electrical tape to secure the electrical cord for the lights down the back of the tree. Cover the cord completely with the ribbon.
• To cover the topiary trunk in style, trim it with wide ribbon. Tie two long pieces of ribbon around the lowest part of the trunk. Wrap both pieces of ribbon toward each other in opposite directions. Cross the two ribbons and reverse the direction to meet on the other side of the trunk. Continue in this manner until the bark is concealed.
• Add large bows at the base of the topiary.

garden-theme garland

This rustic salute to the season is best suited to a covered entryway. An important plus for this design is that many of its components can be used year after year.

To make the terra-cotta bells featured on this garland, knot one end of a bundle of raffia (about 10-12 strands); thread the other end through a 4-inch pot and knot. Thread raffia through a 6-inch pot; knot again. For large bells, repeat the procedure with 6-inch and 8-inch pots. Next, make a fan of wheat stalks and secure it with florist wire. Look for garland materials at crafts and import stores.

For the garland centerpiece, wire together a wheat fan, several dried blooms, such as sunflowers or hydrangeas, and the raffia ties of two small bells; then wire on a large bell. Conceal the wire with raffia.

Insert large nails or cup hooks around the door frame. Wire vine, such as kudzu, grape, or honeysuckle, to the nails. Wrap an evergreen garland around the vine, securing it with raffia. Tuck in additional dried blooms and greenery sprigs, if desired. Attach the centerpiece to the garland with florist wire. Tie the remaining bells to the garland using the raffia at the top of the bells. Tie the remaining wheat fans to the garland with raffia. Weave raffia into the garland to fill in gaps.

welcoming
wreaths

TAKE A LOOK AT THIS CLASSIC CHRISTMAS DECORATION IN A DOZEN NEW WAYS.

easy ideas for a grand entrance

When there's so much to do, purchasing a ready-made wreath is a real time-saver. You can personalize it by attaching ribbon and greenery as on the wreath pictured here. It's accented with elaeagnus, juniper, possumhaw, and a plaid bow. Lengths of woody grapevine wrap around the front column and across the porch.

decorating ideas for outdoor entrances

• Use ribbons in holiday colors or in shades that coordinate with your home's exterior to add vitality to your outdoor decorations. If your door is protected by a porch or overhang, you can use any kind of ribbon. But if the areas you're decorating are open to the elements, choose a waterproof ribbon made for exterior use.

• To dress up a purchased wreath, clip greenery such as elaeagnus, holly, cedar, juniper, boxwood, smilax, and nandina; collect pinecones and colorful berries. Hang the wreath on your door, and attach the pieces of greenery with florist wire. Use clippers to shape and trim excess foliage or twigs. Make a bow, and wire it to the wreath.

Work shorter cuttings of other materials under the ribbon and among the longer pieces of greenery.

• Choose a large container to serve as a base for a distinctive arrangement beside the door. Fill the pot with plants such as autumn fern and white ornamental kale, and insert 3- and 4-foot branches into the center to give the arrangement height. (The berried branches in the container shown at right are possumhaw.) Encircle the container with slender grapevines. Then add color by inserting the berries of holly or nandina among the vines.

dried hydrangea wreath

This wreath takes advantage of the fluffy blooms of hydrangeas clipped at their peak in mid to late summer. (See the tips at right for drying cut blooms.) For a wreath that you can use year after year, place permanent hydrangea blooms on a permanent evergreen wreath. Permanent materials can be found at crafts and discount stores.

To make this wreath, use florist wire to attach hydrangea blooms, stems of lemon leaves, and seeded eucalyptus to an evergreen wreath. Add additional materials, as desired. If you use dried blooms, this decoration is best suited to a covered area.

drying hydrangeas

• Mophead, peegee, and oakleaf hydrangeas are particularly well suited for drying. Mophead varieties yield deep blue, purple, and pink blooms that dry to mellowed hues of these colors; peegee and oakleaf blooms dry to brown and burgundy.

• Cut the blooms from the bush after they have begun to dry naturally; the petals should have begun to stiffen slightly. (Picking too soon results in wilted blooms.)

• Always pick more than you think you'll need; some blooms will not dry as successfully as others.

• Strip all of the leaves from the stems.

• Bundle the stems in groups of three or four, and hang them upside down in a dry, dark place for several weeks to dry.

• Once dry, lightly spray the blooms with an inexpensive aerosol hair spray to prevent the blooms from deteriorating.

wreath basics
craft your own greenery wreath

materials
craft foam wreath • evergreen clippings
florist picks

1 Attach greenery clippings to the florist picks. To hold the greenery securely, wrap the wire once around the pick and stem; then bring the wire between the stem and the pick and wrap it around the pick.

2 Wrap the florist wire around both the stem and the pick several more times; then continue wrapping the wire down the length of the pick.

3 Insert "picked" greenery along the inside, outside, and down the center of the wreath form. Work in the same direction all the way around the wreath, and insert the picks at an angle to the wreath form. As you insert the stems along the top of the form, angle them to the left, right, and center, so that the finished wreath will have a balanced fullness.

pinecone wreath

A simple presentation has heartwarming charm in this rustic pine wreath.
Start with an evergreen wreath, or stick pine boughs into a grapevine
wreath, covering it completely. Wrap florist wire around pinecones, and
use the wire to attach the cones to the wreath. Knot a silky ribbon around
the top of the wreath for the hanger.

pecan wreath

A wreath is a grand way to use pecans—a celebrated Southern icon. The wreath shown here begins with a straw wreath form. Cover the form with sheet moss, attached with florist wire. Hot-glue pecans to cover the form, allowing bits of moss to peek through. Tie a ribbon around the top of the wreath to use as a hanger.

a wreath within a wreath

Add interest to a plain evergreen wreath by placing a smaller wreath (intertwined pepperberry and grapevine are shown here) inside the larger one.
Connect the two with thin wire or fishing line. Use ribbon for the hanger.

bright berry wreath

Making your own wreath will put you in the mood for the holidays. This one is easy to make because it uses a purchased grapevine wreath as its base.

For the wreath, insert clusters of nandina berries to cover the grapevine wreath. Use florist wire to hold the berries in place; they will still hang a little loose. Once the berries are in place, use the same method to attach fruit (with stems attached when available). We used clementines, lemons, and kumquats. If you can't find fruit with stems, insert florist picks into the fruit, and secure the picks into the wreath.

We recommend hanging the wreath in a stationary position so as not to disturb the berries, which tend to fall a bit when shaken.

holly berry wreath

Create unexpected drama by foregoing the greenery and letting this simple wreath of stemmed red berries echo the stark beauty of the wintry season.

To make the wreath, cover a straw wreath with sheet moss, securing the moss with florist wire. Using florist wire, bind together three or four stems of either fresh or permanent berries to form a bundle. (For the wreath pictured, we used nine bundles.) Permanent berries are available at crafts and discount stores.

Wire the bundles in place around the wreath, overlapping the bundles so they all face the same direction. Use florist wire to attach a bow.

gardener's wreath

Savor the season with a wreath that showcases the colors and textures of nature. Using a grapevine wreath as the base for this wreath makes it a simple design to assemble.

Gather clippings of assorted evergreens such as cedar, juniper, boxwood, and pine, and tuck them into the grapevine wreath, covering the wreath entirely. Loosely wrap lengths of vine such as grape, kudzu, or honeysuckle around the wreath, securing the vine by pushing its ends into the wreath.

Wire embellishments such as berries, flower bulbs, feathers, and fruit to the wreath. To secure fruit to the wreath, thread florist wire through the fruit and twist the ends of the wire around the wreath form.

Finish the design with a bow, wired to the wreath with florist wire.

magnolia charm

Display the traditional symbol of greeting and goodwill with a wreath made from magnolia leaves—a Deep South favorite. Here, holly berries and hemlock are added to the greenery. Take advantage of outdoor ornamentation, such as this plaque, when planning wreath placement.

making a magnolia wreath
style a classic decoration

Choose magnolia leaves with your particular project in mind. "Little Gem" magnolia is a good selection for small leaves. The leaves of "Majestic Beauty," a large-leaved selection, are perfect for filling an out-of-use fireplace or crafting a garland.

materials

plastic-covered straw wreath form or craft foam wreath • magnolia leaves • U-shaped florist pins

1 Cover the outside edge of the wreath form with the longest leaves, using florist pins to secure them. Overlap the stem of the first leaf with the tip of the next, and use a single pin to hold both in place. After the outside edge of the wreath is covered, pin individual leaves to the top, staggering them along the form and angling one to the inside, one to the outside, and one along the center.

2 Insert the pin at an angle, rather than straight down into the wreath. Work in this manner all the way around the wreath. To finish, tuck the stems of the last leaves under the tips of the first ones.

the secret to fresh foliage

If magnolia is abundant, you may choose to refresh your arrangements during the holiday season. Out of water, the thick leaves remain fresh for about five days; then they begin to dry and curl (which can be very attractive, as well). Placed in water, they last significantly longer. Here are a few tips to maximize longevity.

• Take a bucket of warm water into the garden along with very sharp pruners. Make the cut at a sharp angle, and place foliage immediately into the container.

• Once indoors, recut the woody stems and soak them overnight in fresh water.

• When using magnolia in an arrangement, put stems in a vase or moist florist foam to keep them fresh.

twice the charm

Craft a double wreath to hang in a small window or on a drawer pull or door knob. To create the arrangement, use heavy-gauge florist wire to make two circular shapes—one smaller than the other. Clip nandina berries, and gently attach them to the wreaths with lightweight florist wire. Join with ribbon, and make a bow for hanging.

initial wreath

Personalize a wreath and make it uniquely yours. Draw or trace the letter of your choice onto a piece of paper. On a photocopier, enlarge the letter to the desired size. Cut out the letter to use as a pattern.

Using the pattern, trace the letter onto a sheet of craft foam. Cut out the letter from the craft foam using a sharp knife. Cover the foam shape with sheet moss, using U-shaped florist pins or florist wire to hold the moss in place; or hot-glue the moss onto the shape, if you prefer. Pin or glue a length of ribbon to the back of the wreath for a hanger. Embellish the wreath with ribbon as desired, pinning or gluing it to secure it to the wreath.

ornament wreath

Fashion a decoration from well-loved collectibles such as the ornaments in this wreath. Wherever it's displayed during the holidays, it's sure to be appreciated. Begin with a straw wreath form. Tie a ribbon around the form to serve as a hanger. Hot-glue the ornaments in layers onto the form. Apply plenty of adhesive to each one, and allow it to cool and dry completely before adding another. Work the ornaments like a puzzle; place the largest pieces first, and fill in around them with smaller ones.

stacked wreaths

herald the season with a luxuriant topiary of layered evergreens and fruit

Give a natural look to your home's front door with an unusual accent made from wreaths of fruit and evergreen foliage. The topiary pictured is about 5 feet tall and requires six wreath forms for greenery and four forms for the fruit. The bottom wreath is a few inches larger in diameter than the opening of the container.

Greenery for this topiary was attached to wreath forms that range in diameter from 18 inches at the bottom to 8 inches at the top. (If a variety of sizes is unavailable, add extra greenery to a small wreath form to make it appear larger.) Large red apples were attached to a 16-inch straw wreath form. Oranges, lemons, and small green apples were attached to 12-inch wreath forms.

Once you've made the wreaths, simply stack them to form the topiary, starting with the largest rings of foliage and fruit, then moving to the top, adding wreaths that decrease in size. Stabilize the wreaths with wire, if desired.

materials

plastic-wrapped straw wreath forms
greenery cuttings • clippers • florist wire
and pins • fresh fruit • 6-inch wooden
florist picks • container
square piece of wood

1 Purchase wreaths or make them yourself, using evergreen clippings. For small wreaths, cut the greenery about 5 inches long; make the pieces a few inches longer for larger wreaths. Cluster several pieces of greenery together, and bind them with florist wire. Attach the greenery clusters to the straw wreath form with florist pins. All the greenery clusters should be turned in the same direction. Cover the form thickly, so that each wreath will stand at least 4 inches high. The topiary pictured uses six evergreen wreaths.

2 To make a fruit wreath, attach fresh fruit to the outside edge of a straw wreath form. Insert one end of a florist pick into the piece of fruit and the other end into the straw wreath form. Continue attaching fruit until the outside edge of the wreath is completely covered. The topiary pictured uses four fruit wreaths.

3 Place a square of wood on top of the container. Set the largest wreath of greenery on top of the wood, then add a wreath of fruit. Continue adding wreaths, alternating greenery and fruit. Place two small wreaths of greenery at the top. Fill in at the top of the topiary and around the top of the container with magnolia.

a gallery
of garlands

EXPRESS THE ESSENCE OF HOLIDAY SPIRIT
WITH BEAUTIFUL, BOUNTIFUL SWAGS.

being natural

Fresh fragrances and textures of boughs of evergreens and citrus fruits,
and the cheery reds of holly and nandina berries are holiday embellishments that exude the joys of the season.

When using natural materials, put up your outdoor decorations no
sooner than two weeks before Christmas to keep them looking fresh
through the holiday. Indoor swags and garlands are affected by central
heating and will benefit from a misting with water every few days.

The garland and wreaths shown here are resplendent because they
blend so well with the natural setting. The ribbon trim adds a festive
look but doesn't overwhelm the subtle charm of the gracefully swagged
arrangement.

guide to garlands

• Purchase a cedar garland from a
florist or Christmas tree lot, and
hang it from a window, door, or banister for a quick-and-easy decoration. Cedar's simple charm will
create a cozy atmosphere.

• To hang a garland over a window
or door, insert small nails into the
molding above. Use florist wire to attach the garland to the nails, and let
it drape to the floor.

• For a bold garland embellishment,
envelop plump welting (found at fabric stores) in red velvet. Cut velvet

strips wide enough to wrap around the welting (ends should overlap 1 inch). Stitch the
short ends of the strips together to form a long strip. Fold the long strip around the welting. Turn ½ inch to the underside and hand-stitch the fold into place. Wrap the velvet
rope around a garland or banister, or use it to trim your tree.

a garland from the garden

This door decor consists of a luxurious pine swag embellished with raffia, ribbon, pinecones, miniature baskets, and small terra-cotta pots. Florist wire holds the add-ons in place.

⭐ **MEASURE UP** Use a tape measure to estimate the length of garland you'll need. Allow for an extra yard of garland to spiral to the floor on each side.

making a garland
this easy technique uses a slender rope as the base for the evergreen

Start with a piece of rope the length you want the garland to be, and anchor one end so that you can hold the rope taut as you work.

materials
rope or clothesline • 6-inch-long greenery clippings • florist wire (on a spool)

1 Wrap one end of the wire near the anchored end of the rope to secure it, then lay one or two cuttings along the rope and wrap tightly with wire. Do not cut the wire.

2 Place another bundle of two or three cuttings on the opposite side of the rope and wrap with wire, pulling the wire tightly to secure the cuttings to the rope. Lay a third group along the clothesline so that its foliage generously covers the wire and stems of the first two; spiral the wire down to the stems of this group and wrap them securely to the clothesline.

3 Continue wiring bundles of cuttings to the rope, keeping all stems pointing in the same direction and wrapping the wire as tightly as possible. To make sure the garland is well shaped and full, continue attaching cuttings so that bunches extend to the left, right, and center all the way around the rope.

When you reach the end, hide the stems with bundles of cuttings attached so that the stems point in the opposite direction. Work these stems into the foliage to hide them. Cut off excess rope at each end.

clip tips

When you cut foliage, remember you are actually pruning the plant. Though late winter is the best time to prune, mid-December, when evergreens are dormant, is not too early. By making garlands and other holiday decorations, you have the opportunity to actually use the foliage you prune.

The way you make a cut will determine how a shrub or tree will re-grow. Study the plant to determine where to prune to leave it looking well balanced. Try not to cut a major branch from any plant. When cutting a boxwood, snip away a little here and a little there to open up the plant so that sunlight will filter down through the leaves. Before using foliage, condition it by soaking it in water overnight.

collectible charm

Sometimes the best use for a garland is as a background for other decorations. The mantel at right shows how the garland fills in nicely around collections of nutcrackers and whimsical ornaments. Tiny white lights scattered along the mantel create twinkling reflections in the gold star garland.

inviting elegance

An evergreen garland wrapped with wired ribbon gracefully festoons the mantelpiece and fills the room with the unmistakable scent of cedar. Floral wire secures the ribbon and bow.

Here a deep firebox keeps flames well away from the greenery, something to keep in mind when placing decorations near a fireplace or candle.

holiday harvest

'Tis the season to make the most of pruning. Here are guidelines to help with the holiday harvest.

Beautyberry: This native shrub loses its leaves by December, so the vivid purple berries are your target. Clip berry-laden branches back as far as you want, but don't remove more than one-third of them. There's no need to place the branches in water; the berries last a long time without it.

Bittersweet: Like beautyberry, this vine loses its leaves early on. Clip long lengths of the berried stems. No need to place them in water; the red berries last for months indoors. But handle the branches gently—the showy yellow husks attached to the berries are brittle and break easily.

Boxwood: Reach inside the shrub and cut sections 6 to 8 inches long. Prune from various spots around the plant to maintain the natural, billowy appearance. Always cut back to green growth. Condition the cuttings by immersing them in cold water for 24 hours prior to use.

Japanese aucuba: This shrub is prized for its yellow-and-green variegated foliage. As with holly, prune to shape the shrub. Cut back to a crotch or dormant bud. Immerse in water for 24 hours to condition. The foliage lasts about a week out of water.

Nandina: Huge berry clusters atop this shrub can't be beat. Cut leggy stalks back to foliage lower down in the plant. No need for conditioning; the bright red berries will last months without it.

Holly: Holly offers glossy, green foliage and bright red berries. Clip branches of any length to shape up the plant. The remaining branch will sprout again from the point of the cuts. Immerse cut branches in water for 24 hours to condition.

ornamented with roses

Hundreds of dried miniature spray roses fill garlands
(above) that frame the fireplace and mantel. After
the holidays, the roses can be removed from the garlands and used in other arrangements or stored away
safely for next Christmas.

a grand statement

Abundant boxwood garlands frame the doorways
that lead through the house (right). They are
adorned with pinecones, pomegranates, gold ribbon,
gilded baby artichokes, ornamental angels, roses,
and hydrangea blooms.

SMART SHOPPING The produce department is a marvelous place to find some seasonal decorations.
Pomegranates, lemons, limes, kumquats, and cranberries offer rich color. Artichokes and Granny Smith apples
lighten up the green palette. Use them in garlands and wreaths, on the mantel, and in table decorations.

gold and glittery

This garland (left) has such appeal it can be the star of your holiday show. To make the garland, stagger the stems of gold holly and the fruit pieces, and wire or tape them together with brown florist tape. (All materials are available from crafts and discount stores.) Continue until you have the desired length of garland. A 7-foot garland uses eight large stems of holly and fruit. (The holly stems used for the one shown here have several branches coming from the main stem.)

Wire on your choice of berry clusters, ornaments, and assorted embellishments. Add bows along the length of the garland.

berry garland

This twiggy decoration (below) is a suitable adornment all winter long. To make the garland, stagger the stems of red berry sprays (available at crafts and discount stores), and wire or tape them together with brown florist tape. For a 7-foot garland, we used ten stems of berry sprays. (A spray has several thin branches with berries coming from one main stem.)

mantel magic

joyful words

Make a bold literal statement of your love for the season by fashioning greenery-embellished letters to spell out a holiday sentiment. Cut plywood or particleboard into the shape of each letter. Top the wood with water-soaked florist foam. Wrap chicken wire around the foam and the wood base to hold the foam in place. Cover the foam with greenery clippings. (Misting the greenery every few days will keep it looking fresh throughout the holidays.)

For letters you can reuse, cut letters from a sheet of craft foam. Cover the craft foam with sheet moss (use glue, florist wire, or florist pins to attach the sheet moss). Push sprigs of silk greenery and berries into the form. For a hanger, make a loop from decorative cording, and secure the ends on the back of the letter.

The mantel scarf is made by layering napkins. The tassels are held with double-faced mounting tape.

cheery accents

Red candles and berries set a bright mood on this mantel. Branches of berries stand tall in urns that frame the setting, while the delicate raspberry wreath adds interest at the center of the arrangement.

To make the wreath, cover a wreath form with sheet moss. The wreath shown here is approximately 9 inches in diameter. Hot-glue a variety of artificial or dried berries to the wreath. For a hanger, loop a ribbon around the wreath, and add a bow in front, if desired.

polka-dot jewel candles

On the mantel, nestle pillar candles in stair-step heights among the greenery of a garland. Place the tallest candle first and arrange the others from that point. Add some ornaments and kumquats to the mix, tucking them around the candles at assorted angles.

To make polka-dot candles, hot-glue glass beads (the kind with flat backs) to pillar candles, arranging the beads in a diamond pattern. Hold each bead in place until secure.

⭐ **COLORFUL CHOICES** For the polka-dot jewel candles, clear gems on a white candle look rather elegant, while red or green have a more whimsical appeal.

tulip surprise

Nestled into an evergreen garland, clear glass cylinders show off bright tulip blooms. For each cylinder, put ½ cup of clear marbles in the cylinder. Gently work a tulip stem into the marbles, and carefully drop another ½ cup of clear marbles around the base to hold the flower securely in place. Slowly drizzle water down the cylinder's side, filling it just above the top of the flower.

The tulips will last three to four days. Add green apples and white candles to the mantel arrangement for the finishing touch.

For a similar look with longer life, add water to cover only the marbles. The tulips will not deteriorate as rapidly, but will continue to grow. Add some water every day, and trim the stems to keep the blossoms confined within the vase.

decorate with stockings

Use stockings as the main theme of your mantel display. Cover the mantel with a mantel scarf, if desired (see the easy-to-do mantel scarf on page 54). Line up the stockings in soldier fashion along the mantel. To keep the stockings upright, weight them with small bags of black-eyed peas (that you can put to good use on New Year's Day!). Fill the stockings with small toys, tiny wrapped packages, and candy canes.

WORK WITH NATURE To give stockings decorative impact—whether they're placed on the mantel (as above) or hanging in the traditional way—fill them with cuttings of fir, cedar, elaeagnus, and other types of greenery. Tie ribbons to the hanging loops and let them drape down the sides of the stockings.

personal favorites

Supplement your customary display of Christmas decorations with some of your favorite accessories. Select objects that lend different shapes and textures to the setting such as the birdhouse and Staffordshire dogs in the arrangement shown above. Greenery and candles help convey the holiday spirit.

children's choice

Use a youthful collection of small toys and tiny stuffed animals as trimmings for a garland of fresh greenery. Add an appealing splash of color by filling glass jars with peppermints, candy canes, and gum-drops. Insert lollipops and other cellophane-wrapped sweets into potted plants.

down-home style

Three small vine wreaths hang from a band of twigs. The twig band can be purchased from a crafts store, or you can wire together twigs that you find scattered in your back-yard. Decorate the vine wreaths with an assortment of berries, greenery, even small pieces of fruit, nuts, and pinecones attached with florist wire, florist picks, or a hot-glue gun. Wire the wreaths to the twig band, then cover the wire with a crisp bow.

a mantel in minutes
step-by-step to a classic look

Your mantel can come together in no time. Use fabulous magnolia foliage to make an elegant backdrop for other holiday elements.

materials
magnolia branches • candles
red berries • ribbon

1 Fill the mantel with freshly cut magnolia branches, ranging from 5 to 10 inches in length.

2 Add candles to the mix, using odd numbers and varying heights.

3 Tuck clusters of nandina, holly, or other berries among the magnolia.

4 Trail metallic ribbon among the branches to weave it all together.

flower garden inspirations

Let your everyday decor suggest your holiday trimmings. A rich flower garden painting above this mantel inspires a bounty of rosebuds, clusters of nandina berries, and even ornamental cabbages atop a greenery garland that puddles on the floor amidst pots of poinsettias. For holiday entertaining, go all out with vases of red roses at each end of the mantel (or use poinsettias for a less expensive option). Red and green velvet stockings rival the roses' sumptuousness.

snowy scene

Dreams of a white Christmas come true with the frosty combination of
white and silver. White pillar candles and white, clear, and silver containers
set the wintry mood. Angel hair creates a soft cloud along the top of the
mantel. Large white snowflakes and pearl-white ornaments are suspended
by ribbons at varying lengths, giving an interesting finish. Topiaries are
made by hot-gluing small ornaments to a tree form.

fast-and-easy stockings
go from plain to perky with dressy trims

Each of these stockings was purchased for just a couple of dollars at a drugstore. For the first two stockings, we removed the fur cuff and added a new design. For the third one, we just glued on some sparkly embellishments. Try the ideas we describe here, or use these photographs as inspiration for your own fancy look.

ribbon cuff

materials

stocking • 3 yards (1½-inch-wide) wired black gingham ribbon • glue • jingle bells • 1¼ yards (1½-inch-wide) wired red ribbon • liquid ravel preventer • 2 yards (1-inch-wide) embroidered ribbon • 18-inch length of gold trim

1 Cut the cuff off at the top of the stocking. Cut the black gingham ribbon into 10-inch lengths. Fold each length in half, forming a loop. Place the ribbon loops side by side, aligning the raw edges with the top of the stocking. Glue the ribbons in place. Using a doubled length of black thread, tie one small jingle bell to the ribbon at the center fold.

2 Cut red ribbon into 3½-inch lengths. Place one raw edge of each ribbon length along the top of the stocking, aligning the ribbon lengths side by side. Glue the ribbons in place. Apply liquid ravel preventer to the loose end of each ribbon length. Let dry.

3 Cut embroidered ribbon into 3-inch lengths, trimming one end to a point. Apply liquid ravel preventer to the pointed end. Let dry. Place the ribbon lengths side by side, aligning the straight edges with the top of the stocking. Add or overlap pieces to create the desired fullness in the fringe. Glue in place. Glue gold trim along the top edge of the stocking, covering the raw edges of the ribbons.

4 Make a bow, and attach it to the wreath with wire. Next, work shorter cuttings of other natural materials underneath the ribbon and among the longer pieces of greenery.

MORE IDEAS For a whimsical look, use several different-colored ribbons and buttons on your stockings. Mix and match gingham with polka-dotted trims. Sew on miniature ornaments instead of bells.

button cuff

materials
stocking • fabric remnant for cuff and hanger • buttons

1 Cut the cuff off at the top of the stocking. From the fabric remnant, cut a 7-inch-wide piece that will fit around the top edge of the stocking and overlap slightly. Also from the fabric remnant, cut a 2- by 10-inch strip for the hanging loop.

2 With the wrong sides together, fold the fabric for the cuff in half lengthwise, creasing it at the fold. Tuck the top half of the folded fabric piece into the top of the stocking, aligning the center fold along the top of the stocking and overlapping the fabric edges. Glue the fabric on the inside of the stocking. Turn the fabric on the outside of the stocking under at the bottom edge and glue to the stocking, forming a finished edge.

3 For the hanging loop, fold the long edges of the fabric strip toward the center. Glue the edges in place. Fold the fabric strip in half with the glued edges on the inside of the loop. Tuck the raw ends of the loop inside the stocking cuff. Glue it in place. Sew buttons along the bottom of the cuff.

holly & tassel cuff

materials
stocking • 18-inch cording with tassel ends • glue wire cutters • gold berry floral picks • silk holly-and-berry floral picks

1 Make a hanging loop by doubling the cording. Knot the cord. Glue the knot to the outside of the cuff at the seam.

2 Use wire cutters to cut gold berries from floral picks. Glue the berries onto the stocking cuff as desired. Cut silk holly leaves and berries from floral picks. Arrange the leaves and berries around the knot in the cord. Glue them in place.

our favorite trees

THE MOST IMPORTANT DECORATION OF THE SEASON?
THE TREE, OF COURSE. ON THESE PAGES, WE SHARE OUR TOP TEN.

traditions rule

Decorating the Christmas tree is a combination of family memories and personal style. As the trees on these two pages show, you can't go wrong loading on all of your treasured ornaments—that's what makes the tree uniquely yours.

We've selected some of our most special trees to spark ideas for new ways to adorn the holiday's classic symbol. Here are a few suggestions.

• Make your tree shine even brighter by lining the trunk with a strand of larger bulb lights. They look like old-fashioned outdoor bulbs, but many can be

used inside. Check the package to be sure the bulbs you buy are for indoor use.

• Ribbon makes a terrific tree garland. Since yards of ribbon can be expensive, use 4-foot lengths and tuck each end into the tree so it looks as if it winds throughout. Strips of fabric or colored burlap work well, too, for a more casual look.

• Instead of a wire hanger, thread a thin ribbon through the loop of an ornament, and tie the ornament to a branch. It will hang more securely on the tree—an especially good idea for fragile ornaments.

christmas trees 101

Buy a fresh tree. To check, shake the tree or run your hand over a branch; if lots of needles fall off, the tree has dried out.

Saw off the bottom inch of the trunk to allow the tree to absorb water. If the tree stand runs out of water before the tree is decorated, trim the trunk again.

Keep the tree moist. Use a tree stand that holds at least a half gallon of water.

Keep it cool. Place your tree away from any heat sources, including sunlight.

Light it right. Use only UL-approved lights. Do not overload the circuits. Never use candles around any type of greenery.

lights
After the tree is in place, it's time to add the lights. Plug the lights in before you start to string them through the tree. An outlet strip can accommodate up to 15 amps. The single switch makes turning the lights on and off more convenient.

When the time comes to take down the tree, don't just pull off all the lights and stuff them in a box. Instead, remove each strand separately and carefully wrap around a piece of corrugated cardboard.

ornaments
Take extra care in hanging ornaments. Wire hooks are usually safe if placed over a substantial branch. Valuable or heavy ornaments are best tied in place with ribbon. After the holidays, store your ornaments in their original boxes or in special cardboard containers.

tree disposal
After all the ornaments and lights are removed, wrap the tree in an old sheet or use a disposable plastic tree bag to remove the tree from the house. That way you won't leave a trail of evergreen needles and tinsel on the floor. After removing the tree, take it to a recycling center where old trees are ground into mulch.

a good fit

Consider the scale of the room with regard to the tree as if you were selecting new furniture. Measure the floor area before you buy. A 4- by 4-foot space will gracefully accommodate a slender 6- to 7-foot tree.

Find the perfect spot in the house so everyone can enjoy the color and lights. Placing the tree in the foyer, like the one shown here, allows family and guests to appreciate your most outstanding decoration as soon as they enter.

take a stand

Having the right tree stand helps get your tree trimming started on a positive note. Here are suggestions to make this holiday task a little more enjoyable.

• Take your tree stand along when you go shopping for a tree; that way you can check the fit before you buy.

• When buying a tree stand, choose one that can accommodate a trunk up to 5 inches in diameter.

• Select a stand that can hold at least a half gallon of water. Otherwise, you'll spend a lot of time moving presents out of the way to water the tree.

• A stand that will help your tree stand up straight is important. At a minimum it should have three or four screws around the collar to let you adjust the tree until it's perpendicular. (It also helps if you choose a tree with a straight trunk.) The stand should have a wide enough base to keep the tree from tipping over. Look for legs or a base that's at least 18 inches across.

family favorites

A tree filled with treasured ornaments that are used year after year,
handmade paper cutouts made by
the children in the family, and
swags of colorful beads and ribbons is perhaps the best kind of
decoration. Paper cones filled with
tulips are an unexpected delight on
the tree shown here. The plump
bow at the top enhances the jolly
theme.

   To make a paper cone, cut a rectangle from construction paper.
Roll the paper into a loose cone;
trim the top with scissors to make
a straight edge. Secure with double-sided tape. For the handle,
punch a hole on each side of the
cone, and thread a ribbon through
the holes. Knot the ribbon ends
on the outside of the cone. Florist
picks filled with water keep each
flower fresh as it rests in the cone.

HOLIDAY HOW-TO

easy classic bow
wire bows together to make a big impression

Top your tree with a festive bow, using the directions below; then just wire individual bows together to make a grand topper for your tree. Our bow is 6 inches wide and uses 2 yards of ribbon. For larger bows, add ½ yard of ribbon for every 2-inch increase.

materials
2 yards (1½-inch-wide) double-faced ribbon • tape measure • florist wire

1 Cut one (18-inch) length of ribbon; set aside. Beginning and ending with 6-inch tails, fold the remaining ribbon into six (6-inch) loops as shown, pinching ribbon together in the center. Wire the loops in the center to hold the ribbon in place.

2 Loosely knot the center of the 18-inch ribbon. Centering the knot over the wire at the center of the bow, tie the ribbon around the wired loops.

trimming tips

• Place lights on the tree first, then add bead garlands or ribbon. Hang ornaments last so they can be distributed evenly.
• Apply lights to the tree by threading each branch with a back and forth motion until you've gone around the tree. This prevents the lights from overlapping, and they're much easier to remove.
• Look for inexpensive bead garlands at discount and home-center stores.
• Update an old favorite by lightly spray painting popcorn garlands with gold paint.
• Alternate colored ornaments throughout the tree for diversity.
• Tie several groups of three inexpensive ball ornaments together for impact, and hang the clusters throughout the tree.
• Tiny packages tucked into the tree will fill any holes in the branches and will add to the holiday anticipation.
• For the crowning glory, ribbons and bows finish off the top just as well as a star or an angel. If you can't tie a big bow yourself, ask your local florist to make one (or try our directions for an easy classic bow, above). Using a variety of colorful ribbons in the bow helps create impact. Weave the long tails into the tree, and the bow will unify all the ribbons interlaced within the branches.
• Decorate only one side of a corner tree, which requires less ornaments, lights, and time. Tie any corner tree so it won't fall from the weight of the concentrated trimmings.

indoor garden

Bring the look of a cottage garden to the Christmas evergreen with hand-made ornaments, a picket fence, and pails of bright green grass.

For the grass, fold ryegrass seed into potting soil. Arrange pebbles in a pail. Fill the pail three-fourths full with the seeded soil, and sprinkle a heavy layer of seed on top. Place the pail in a sunny spot, and water it regularly. The seed will sprout in about ten days.

garden-inspired ornaments

violet bouquet Hold together the stems of silk violets and arrange silk leaves around the flowers. Wrap the stems together with florist tape. Tie a ribbon around the taped stems. Tuck the bouquet among the tree branches.

garden accents Using tracing paper, transfer the pattern on page 248 to a sheet of craft foam. Cut out the ornament. To make the hanger, pierce the ornament at the center top with a pencil tip or other pointed object; thread a length of gold craft wire through the hole and knot the ends together.

petite pots Fill a 2-inch terra-cotta pot with florist foam. Press three to four small dried roses with stems into the foam, leaving a small space in the center. For the hanger, fold a length of raffia in half and knot the ends together. Attach the knotted end of the raffia to the foam at the center. Press tiny dried leaf stems into the foam, filling in around the roses and the hanger.

kissing ball Trim the stems of dried flowers to 2 inches (we used dried hydrangeas). Push the stems into a craft foam ball. Continue until the ball is almost covered, leaving a small uncovered spot to attach the hanger. For the hanger, fold a ribbon in half and knot the ends together. Attach the ribbon loop to the ball using a florist pin. Hot-glue the ribbon hanger to secure it.

natural selection

Some of the best decorating ideas come from nature. A fine example is this commanding Fraser fir, which is trimmed with materials easily found in most backyards. To decorate your tree for a similar look, here are a few suggestions.

• String on the lights first.

• Weave bittersweet or other similar vine throughout the tree.

• Tuck in clusters of dried oak leaves and twigs in the spaces between the branches.

• Wire on your favorite ornaments.

• Add the final touches. The tree pictured has a tin Christmas star tree topper and a burlap tree skirt to complete the natural look.

decorating naturally

• Before you spend a lot of money buying materials, work with the greenery you probably have in your backyard.

• Fill a glass vase with cut greenery. Add several inches of nandina berries to the vase. Fill with water.

• Cluster pots of paperwhites, amaryllis, or poinsettias in key locations such as on mantels or tables, rather than placing one pot in each room.

trimmed with flowers

Dried flowers and strands of white lights make a unique holiday display. To decorate your tree with dried flowers, first cover the tree with white lights. Use large blooms, such as the dried hydrangea blooms on this tree, to fill in gaps between branches. Next, start at the top of the tree with smaller flowers and work your way down with the larger ones, trying to get an even distribution of shapes, sizes, and colors.

Many small flowers may need to be bunched to make an impact. Cut the stems to different lengths, and secure the stems with florist wire. Cover the stems with florist tape so they won't be visible when you wire them to the tree.

EVERLASTING BEAUTY Hydrangeas, yarrow, statice, roses, and globe amaranth retain their color when dried and are good choices for adorning your tree.

harvest tree
fill your tree with bountiful baskets and berries

Baskets spilling with fruit add motion and whimsy to this tree's homespun good looks.

blackberry ornament
materials
*raffia • canning jar rings • hot-glue gun and glue sticks
artificial blackberry sprigs*

1 Make a tassel by doubling strands of raffia. Wrap and tie a piece of raffia around the top to create the "head" of the tassel. Clip any leftover wrapped raffia, and dab the tie with hot glue to secure.

2 Glue two canning jar rings together to make the frame of the ornament.

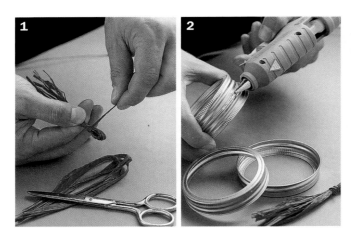

3 Tie two pieces of raffia together at each end (this makes the raffia easier to hold). Wrap the raffia around the outside edge of the canning jar rings, securing with glue in at least four spots. Thread a piece of raffia through what you've just secured and tie it off to make a hanger for the ornament.

4 Place a sprig of blackberries to the side of the ring. Hot-glue the fruit to the rings. Cover spots of glue with leaves. Place a dot of glue inside the top of the rings. Press the tassel into the glue to secure. Let dry.

tips for a bountiful tree

• Place white icicle lights in the tree's interior to add shimmer.

• For the garland, wind split strands of gold burlap into the tree, starting at the top and placing it deep among the branches.

• For the tree topper, insert sticks of curly willow spray painted gold and copper.

• Tie baskets filled with excelsior (or shredded paper) and plastic fruit to the tree with raffia. (Floral wire helps secure the fruit in the baskets.) Tie strands of raffia around the basket handles, allowing ribbons of raffia to cascade from the handle.

• Add ornaments. Bunch fabric at the base of the tree to make the skirt.

BRIGHT IDEA Strands of icicle lights in the lowest branches of the tree add light at the tree's base and intermingle with the stacked gifts.

outdoor elegance

A decorated tree is a warm and welcoming decoration on a covered front porch. The tree is encircled with white lights, grapevine, and garlands of red berries. (Permanent berry garlands, purchased from a crafts store, are used for their bright colors and weather resistance.) Berry-covered spheres hang from the tree's branches. Moss-covered packages are nestled around the base of the tree.

- -

HOLIDAY HOW-TO

easy style
natural materials provide simple style

moss-wrapped packages For moss-wrapped packages, glue sheet moss to a large cardboard box, and tie the bow with wide ribbon. For an additional accent, wire or hot-glue clusters of artificial fruit to the top of the box. Be sure to place the boxes under a covered entry to keep them looking their best.

natural ornaments To make ornaments similar to the cranberry balls on this tree, hot-glue dried fruits, moss, or berries onto craft foam balls, covering the entire ball. Hot-glue a ribbon or twine loop onto the top of the ball to use as a hanger.

- -

fresh fragrance for the tree

A ring of potted poinsettias and dried fruit ornaments add a delicate touch and delightful fragrance to this tree (right). To make the dried citrus ornaments, follow these easy tips.

• Arrange sliced citrus fruit on a wire rack. Place the rack on a baking sheet, and bake the fruit at 200° for six to ten hours, or until it looks leathery. (The time varies depending on the type of fruit, the thickness of the slices, and the humidity.)

• Remove the fruit from the oven, and allow it to finish drying on the rack. It's done when it feels dry to the touch.

• Run a ribbon through the center of each slice, tie, and hang it on the tree.

citrus sensations
add zest to holiday decorations

Like sunshine on a cold winter's day, circles of dried citrus evoke warm sentiments. Make the topiary and citrus ornaments to add zing to your seasonal decor.

materials

hot-glue gun and glue sticks • craft foam cone • sheet moss • dried citrus slices stick • florist foam • assorted greenery

1 Hot-glue sheet moss to a craft foam cone, covering the cone. Hot-glue dried citrus slices in rows around the tree. (Directions for drying fruit are on page 82.)

2 Insert a stick into the base of the tree, and secure the topiary in a block of moistened florist foam placed in a decorative container. Fill in around the base with cuttings of ivy, boxwood, or assorted greenery.

clearly beautiful trims

transform glass ornaments into showstopping designs

Create distinctive holiday ornaments by painting or embellishing clear glass ornaments with items found at a crafts or art-supply store. The dragées (silver candy beads) shown on this page can be found at grocery or crafts stores or wherever cake-decorating supplies are sold. You'll find inexpensive clear glass Christmas ornaments at import stores and other shops that sell decorations.

silver bead ornaments

materials

clear glass ornaments • dragées • hot-glue gun and glue sticks

1 Hot-glue dragées to the glass ball in a random design. Let dry.

2 Tie a shimmery ribbon through the hanging loop. (The beads are delicate, so handle the ornaments carefully.)

painted ornaments

materials

clear glass ornaments • enamel paint pens in assorted colors, such as red, green, gold, and copper

1 Draw a shape, such as a star or circle, at the top of the ornament, using an enamel paint pen. Draw lines from the original shape down the sphere to the base of the ornament. Make
the lines curved, straight, or diagonal, depending on the effect
you wish to achieve. For greater visual interest, include a few
smaller shapes at the top or bottom or on other selected areas.

2 Add color by filling in some of the shapes you've drawn.
Rather than completely covering the surface, keep the ornament slightly transparent by letting portions of the clear
glass shine through the paint. When you've filled in the out-
lined areas, emphasize some of the original lines by redrawing
them in a contrasting color.

MAKE A SET Add a brightly colored ribbon tie to each ornament. A boxed set would make a great gift for teachers or neighbors.

petite alternatives

NO ROOM FOR A STANDARD CHRISTMAS TREE? TRY A TINY CONIFER
TO MAKE A BIG STATEMENT IN A LITTLE SPACE.

compact conifers

Take along your container to the garden shop to make the perfect selection of a tiny tree. Spruce, juniper, cypress, and pine are good choices. Dress each pot with moss to hide unsightly edges. Surround the plant's base with ornaments for a splash of color.

stairway style

Small evergreens in red pots line up on the stairs and require no other adornment. Plants this size need water daily; moss helps retain the moisture. To protect furnishings and furniture from moisture, line the containers with saucers, plastic, or foil.

country look

Wrap pots of evergreens with squares of burlap tied in place with twine, and place them on the table for a casual centerpiece. Protect the tabletop by placing the pots in saucers or on plates. A red-and-green plaid tablecloth and two long cedar garlands crisscrossed at the center and draped to the floor reinforce the rustic scene.

packed with surprises

Add an unexpected element by using a container, such as an old suitcase or a wooden crate, that might not ordinarily hold plants at all. In the photo below, a suitcase holds a small forest. White flowers, trailing ivy, and pinecones fill in around the evergreen plants. Protect the container with a layer of plastic or other waterproof material.

conifer care

The best way to keep conifers healthy is to maintain them outdoors, bringing them in only when company comes. But moving decorations back and forth is not always practical, so try these tips.

Water every two to three days. Indoor heat is drying, and a conifer's soil should never dry out. A finger in the dirt will not give you a good reading on dryness; a moisture meter is more helpful.

Keep them cool. Whenever possible, place your arrangements away from sources of heat. This will lessen drying and diminish insect problems.

Watch out for spider mites. Signs of infestation include brown or yellow needles and small webs. Prevention is easier than a cure, so mist the foliage daily with water.

Once the holidays have passed, gently introduce your shrubs back outdoors. Place them outside on warm days, and protect them, in an unheated garage, from frigid nighttime temperatures. Remember to water about once a week. After reconditioning, plant conifers as a group in a large container, or add to your landscape.

tomato cage trees
a festive transformation

Tomato cages become sculptural towers when decorated with greenery, candles, and ribbons. Whether used on a dining room sideboard or nestled in terra-cotta pots beside the front door, they add a whimsical touch.

materials

garden tomato cages • gold spray paint • gold string
fresh greenery branches • hot-glue gun and glue sticks
votive holders and votives • gold cording
clear twinkle lights (optional) • assorted plastic gift
packages and/or fruit • ribbon

1 Paint the tomato cage with gold spray paint. Let dry. Position the cage upside down so the widest tier is at the bottom. Referring to the photograph and using gold string, tie branches of fresh greenery around each tier of the cage. (We used fresh smilax, which stayed fresh-looking indoors for three weeks.)

2 To attach the votive holders, hot-glue the bottoms of the votive holders to the tops of the tomato cage tiers, placing them beside the vertical posts. Let dry. Tie strips of gold cording around the votive holders and posts. (You may use twinkle lights instead of votive holders and votives, if desired. Attach the lights to the tomato cage with florist wire.)

3 To attach the packages or fruit, hot-glue the bottoms and sides of the pieces to the cage. Let dry.

4 To add the ribbon, knot a length of ribbon around the four points at the top of the cage. Tie additional lengths of ribbon to the bow, and let them trail down the sides of the tree.

cut & glue decorations
make a fun felt skirt and ornaments for the tree

Add bright holiday cheer with this brilliant no-sew tree skirt and matching ornaments. This is a project that can include the whole family. Kids will love gluing the Christmas tree forest onto the skirt.

cut & glue tree skirt

materials

patterns on page 249 • tracing paper • 9- by 12-inch felt sheets (We used 4 gold, 4 kelly green, 4 apple green, 8 hunter green, and 4 chartreuse.) • 54-inch-diameter precut red felt circle or 1½ yards of 54-inch-wide red felt • thick craft glue 1⅓ yards of 1-inch-wide gold ribbon

1 Using tracing paper, transfer patterns to felt, and cut out as indicated.

2 If using a precut circle, find the center of the skirt by folding the circle into fourths. Mark and cut out a 6-inch-diameter circle at the center. Cut a straight line from the outer edge to the inner circle for the opening. (If using uncut felt, refer to the cutting diagram and instructions on page 249.)

3 Referring to the photograph for placement, first glue the trees to the skirt, then glue on the stars and moon.

4 For ties, cut four (12-inch) pieces of ribbon. Glue one end each of two ribbons to each side of the opening. Let dry. Tie the ribbons together to close the skirt. The finished skirt is 54 inches in diameter.

cut & glue ornaments

materials

patterns on page 249 • tracing paper 9- by 12-inch felt sheets in assorted holiday colors red and green embroidery floss • embroidery needle

1 For each ornament, using tracing paper, transfer desired pattern to felt, and cut two.

2 With edges aligned, stitch pieces together using embroidery floss. Tie a small bow where the ends of the floss meet.

3 For a hanger, stitch an 8-inch length of floss through the top of the ornament and knot the ends to form a loop.

★ **TIP** One 9- by 12-inch felt sheet is enough to make approximately four ornaments. Felt sheets can be found at fabric and crafts stores.

entertaining

menus • tablescapes • recipes

SWEET POTATO WAFFLES WITH APRICOT SYRUP, MAPLE-PECAN BACON, SPICED FRUIT, AND MIMOSAS

Family Christmas Breakfast

INDULGE IN SOME NEW BREAKFAST DISHES THIS HOLIDAY SEASON. WE'VE GATHERED MIX-AND-MATCH RECIPES FOR ANY OCCASION. TAKE YOUR CHOICE OF WAFFLES, FRENCH TOAST, PANCAKES, OR COFFEE CAKE AS A MAIN DISH, AND SERVE WITH OUR TOP-RATED SIDES AND BEVERAGES.

menu
serves 6 to 8

Sweet Potato Waffles • *Apricot-Stuffed French Toast* • *Orange Bread*

Gingerbread Pancakes • *Maple-Pecan Bacon* • *Spiced Fruit* • *Mimosas* • *Hot Cocoa*

SWEET POTATO WAFFLES

2¼ cups all-purpose flour
 4 teaspoons baking powder
 ¼ cup firmly packed brown sugar
1½ teaspoons ground cinnamon
 ½ teaspoon ground ginger
 4 large eggs, separated
 2 large eggs
 2 cups milk
 1 teaspoon vanilla extract
 1 cup mashed cooked sweet potato
   (1 pound)
 1 cup chopped pistachio nuts
Apricot Syrup (optional; see recipe at right)
Garnish: chopped pistachio nuts

Combine first 5 ingredients in a bowl; make a well in center.

Combine 4 egg yolks, 2 whole eggs, milk, vanilla, and sweet potato; stir into flour mixture just until moistened.

Beat 4 egg whites at high speed with an electric mixer until soft peaks form; gently fold into batter.

Sprinkle 1 tablespoon chopped pistachios on a preheated, lightly greased waffle iron; cover with batter, and bake until crisp. Repeat procedure with remaining pistachios and batter. Serve with Apricot Syrup, and garnish, if desired. Yield: 2 dozen (4-inch) waffles.

APRICOT-STUFFED FRENCH TOAST

 1 (8-ounce) package cream cheese, softened
 ⅓ cup chopped dried apricots
 2 tablespoons sugar
 1 (16-ounce) loaf Italian bread
 4 large eggs
1½ cups half-and-half
 1 teaspoon vanilla extract
Apricot Syrup (optional)

Beat first 3 ingredients at medium speed with an electric mixer until light and fluffy.

Cut ends from bread. Cut bread into 6 thick slices; cut a pocket through top crust of each slice. Stuff each slice with cream cheese mixture; place in a lightly greased 13- x 9-inch baking dish.

Whisk together eggs, half-and-half, and vanilla; pour over bread slices. Cover and chill 30 minutes, turning once.

Cook bread slices on a lightly greased griddle over medium-high heat 3 minutes on all 4 sides or until golden. Serve with Apricot Syrup, if desired. Yield: 6 servings.

apricot syrup:

 1 (10-ounce) jar no-sugar-added apricot spread
 ½ cup maple syrup
 1 teaspoon ground ginger

Stir together all ingredients in a glass bowl. Microwave at HIGH 1 minute. Yield: 1½ cups.

TIP Create a quick centerpiece by placing wrapped packages on the breakfast table. A few twists of the ribbon and some glistening ornaments will add to the festivity.

ORANGE BREAD

¾ cup sugar
½ cup chopped pecans
1 tablespoon grated orange rind
2 (11-ounce) cans refrigerated
  buttermilk biscuits
1 (3-ounce) package cream cheese,
  cut into 20 squares
½ cup butter or margarine, melted
1 cup powdered sugar
2 tablespoons orange juice

Combine first 3 ingredients, and set mixture aside.

Separate each biscuit into 2 halves. Place a cream cheese square between biscuit halves, pressing edges to seal. Dip each biscuit in butter, and dredge in reserved sugar mixture. Stand each biscuit on edge in a lightly greased 12-cup Bundt pan, spacing evenly. Drizzle with remaining butter, and sprinkle with remaining sugar mixture.

Bake at 350° for 45 minutes or until golden. Invert onto a wire rack. Whisk together powdered sugar and orange juice; drizzle over warm bread. Yield: 1 (10-inch) coffee cake.

GINGERBREAD PANCAKES

These pancakes received rave reviews in our Test Kitchens.

1 cup all-purpose flour
1 tablespoon sugar
2 teaspoons baking powder
½ teaspoon salt
1 tablespoon ground cinnamon
½ teaspoon ground ginger
¼ teaspoon ground allspice
⅛ teaspoon ground nutmeg
⅛ teaspoon ground cloves
1 large egg, lightly beaten
1 cup buttermilk
3 tablespoons butter or margarine,
  melted
1 tablespoon molasses
  Orange Marmalade Syrup

Combine first 9 ingredients in a large bowl, and make a well in center of mixture.

Combine egg and next 3 ingredients; add to dry ingredients, stirring just until moistened.

Spoon about 2 tablespoons batter onto a hot, lightly greased griddle. Repeat procedure with remaining pancake batter.

Cook pancakes until tops are covered with bubbles and edges look cooked; turn and cook other side. Serve with Orange Marmalade Syrup. Yield: 10 pancakes.

orange marmalade syrup:

⅔ cup maple syrup
⅓ cup orange marmalade

Combine ingredients in a small saucepan, and bring to a boil, stirring constantly. Yield: 1 cup.

MAPLE-PECAN BACON

Your guests will delight in the salty-sweet combination of bacon drenched in maple syrup and pecans.

16 thick-cut bacon slices
½ cup maple syrup
2 cups finely chopped pecans

Dip bacon in syrup, allowing excess to drain; pat on pecans. Place bacon on a lightly greased rack in a 15- x 10-inch jellyroll pan.

Bake at 400° for 25 minutes; turn and bake 5 more minutes. Yield: 8 servings.

SPICED FRUIT

¾ cup sugar
¾ cup water
6 star anise
3 regular-size orange-and-spice tea
  bags
5 oranges, peeled and sectioned
3 grapefruit, peeled and sectioned
1 fresh pineapple, cored and cubed

Bring first 3 ingredients to a boil in a saucepan; boil, stirring constantly, until sugar dissolves. Remove from heat, and add tea bags; cover and steep 5 minutes. Remove tea bags, squeezing gently, and cool tea.

Remove and discard star anise.

Toss together fruit and tea mixture. Cover and chill 8 hours. Yield: 6 to 8 servings.

MIMOSAS

You can make mock mimosas, if desired. Substitute an equal amount of chilled sparkling water for the champagne.

2 (6-ounce) cans frozen orange juice
  concentrate, thawed and diluted
1 (10-ounce) jar maraschino
  cherries with stems, drained
2 (750-milliliter) bottles dry
  champagne, chilled

Pour half of orange juice into ice cube trays (about 24 cubes); chill remaining juice. Add a cherry to each cube; freeze 8 hours.

Combine champagne and remaining orange juice, and serve immediately over frozen orange juice cubes. Yield: 3 quarts.

HOT COCOA

⅔ cup sugar
½ cup cocoa
  Pinch of salt
1 cup water
8 cups milk
½ teaspoon vanilla extract
  Marshmallows (optional)

Combine first 3 ingredients in a large heavy saucepan. Add water; bring to a boil over medium heat, stirring constantly. Stir in milk; heat thoroughly (do not boil). Stir in vanilla. Serve cocoa immediately with marshmallows, if desired. Yield: 9 cups.

Open House Holiday Brunch

DO YOUR ENTERTAINING A LITTLE DIFFERENT THIS YEAR, AND SERVE A KNOCKOUT OPEN HOUSE BRUNCH TO NEIGHBORS, FRIENDS, AND FAMILY. TAKE OUR RECIPES, MAKE-AHEAD PLAN, AND DECORATING TIPS, AND HAVE A GRAND TIME.

menu
serves 12

Southwestern Egg Casserole • *Cherry Tomato Salad* • *Roasted Red Potato Bites*
Toasted Oat Scones • *Strawberry-Almond Cream Cheese* • *White Sangría Fizz*

SOUTHWESTERN EGG CASSEROLE, ROASTED RED POTATO BITES, AND CHERRY TOMATO SALAD

make-ahead game plan

3 days ahead• Purchase carnations, and make centerpiece for table and wreath for door (see Holiday How-To on page 103).
• Bake Toasted Oat Scones; store in an airtight container.

2 days ahead• Prepare Roasted Red Potato Bites; fill (do not broil) and refrigerate.
• Prepare Strawberry-Almond Cream Cheese; refrigerate.

1 day ahead• Stir together everything except sparkling water for White Sangría Fizz, and refrigerate; add sparkling water just before serving.
• Assemble Southwestern Egg Casserole (do not bake), and refrigerate.

2 hours ahead• Prepare Cherry Tomato Salad; cover and chill.

1 hour ahead• Bake Southwestern Egg Casserole as directed.

20 minutes ahead• Let Roasted Red Potato Bites stand at room temperature 15 minutes; then broil. Warm Toasted Oat Scones.

SOUTHWESTERN EGG CASSEROLE

Assemble this casserole the night before, and bake for 1 hour before guests arrive.

- 12 (5-inch) corn tortillas, cut into 1-inch strips and divided
- 10 large eggs, lightly beaten
- 1 cup half-and-half
- 1 (12-ounce) container 1% low-fat cottage cheese
- ¾ teaspoon salt
- ½ teaspoon pepper
- 1 cup (4 ounces) shredded Mexican cheese blend
- 4 green onions, thinly sliced
- 1½ cups salsa

Place tortilla strips on an ungreased baking sheet.

Bake at 325° for 10 minutes or until crisp; cool.

Whisk eggs in a large bowl; stir in half-and-half and next 3 ingredients. Stir in three-fourths of the tortilla strips, 1 cup cheese, and green onions. Pour mixture into a lightly greased 13- x 9-inch baking dish. Cover with foil, and chill 8 hours.

Bake casserole, covered, at 325° for 40 minutes. Uncover and bake 20 more minutes or just until set. Remove casserole from oven, and let stand 5 minutes. (Casserole will continue to get firm as it cools.)

Cut casserole into 12 squares. Spoon 2 tablespoons salsa over each serving; sprinkle with remaining tortilla strips. Yield: 12 servings.

CHERRY TOMATO SALAD

- 3 pounds cherry tomatoes (about 4 pints), halved and divided
- 2 tablespoons white wine vinegar
- 2 tablespoons olive oil
- 1 teaspoon salt
- ½ teaspoon pepper
- 1 garlic clove, finely chopped
- ¼ cup chopped fresh mint

Stir together first 6 ingredients in a large bowl. Add mint, tossing gently to coat. Cover and chill 1 hour. Yield: 10 to 12 servings.

ROASTED RED POTATO BITES

Transform twice-baked potatoes into irresistible bite-size treats.

- 12 small red potatoes (about 1½ to 2 pounds)
- 1 tablespoon olive oil
- ½ cup mayonnaise
- 1 cup (4 ounces) shredded Cheddar cheese blend
- ½ pound bacon, cooked and crumbled
- ½ cup minced green onions
- 2 tablespoons chopped fresh or 2 teaspoons dried basil

Rub potatoes with olive oil; place on an ungreased baking sheet. Bake at 400° for 45 minutes or until tender. Let cool.

Cut each potato in half crosswise; cut a thin slice from bottom of each half, forming a base for potatoes to stand on, if necessary. Scoop out pulp, leaving at least a ¼-inch-thick shell; reserve pulp.

Stir together reserved potato pulp, ½ cup mayonnaise, Cheddar cheese blend, and remaining 3 ingredients in a large bowl. Spoon or pipe mixture evenly into each potato shell. Place on a lightly greased baking sheet.

Broil potato bites 5 inches from heat 3 to 5 minutes or until lightly browned. Serve warm. Yield: 2 dozen.

Note: Filled, unbroiled potatoes may be covered and chilled up to 2 days. Let stand at room temperature 15 minutes; broil as directed.

TOASTED OAT SCONES

Serve with Strawberry-Almond Cream Cheese (recipe on page 102).

1¼ cups uncooked quick-cooking oats
1½ cups all-purpose flour
½ cup sugar
2 teaspoons baking powder
½ teaspoon salt
½ teaspoon ground cinnamon
¼ teaspoon baking soda
¼ cup butter or margarine, cut up
½ cup sweetened dried cranberries
½ cup fat-free buttermilk
½ cup applesauce
1 teaspoon vanilla extract
2 teaspoons butter or margarine, melted
1 teaspoon sugar

Place oats on a lightly greased baking sheet. Bake at 450° for 3 minutes or until lightly toasted, stirring once. Cool completely.

Combine 1 cup toasted oats, flour, and next 5 ingredients; cut in ¼ cup butter with a pastry blender until crumbly. Add dried cranberries; toss well. Add buttermilk, applesauce, and vanilla, stirring just until dry ingredients are moistened.

Turn dough out onto a lightly floured surface; knead lightly 4 times. Pat dough into a 9-inch circle on a lightly greased baking sheet. Brush with 2 teaspoons melted butter; sprinkle with remaining ¼ cup toasted oats and 1 teaspoon sugar.

Bake at 450° for 11 minutes or until golden. Serve warm. Yield: 12 servings.

ROASTED RED POTATO BITES

TOASTED OAT SCONES

STRAWBERRY-ALMOND CREAM CHEESE

Serve this versatile, hearty cream cheese as a sweet topping for scones, bagels, or English muffins.

1 (8-ounce) package cream cheese, softened
¾ teaspoon almond extract
3 tablespoons powdered sugar
½ cup chopped fresh strawberries (about 8 large strawberries)

Process first 3 ingredients in a food processor just until blended (do not over-process or mixture will be thin). Add strawberries; process just until blended. Cover and chill at least 1 hour. Yield: 1¼ cups.

WHITE SANGRÍA FIZZ

You can serve this Spanish wine beverage over frozen grapes to keep it chilled, if you like.

2 cups fresh orange juice
1 cup sugar
2 (750-milliliter) bottles dry white wine
3 cups sparkling water, chilled
Garnishes: lime, orange, and lemon wedges

Stir together orange juice and sugar in a large pitcher until sugar dissolves. Stir in wine; cover and chill 8 hours.

Stir sparkling water into wine mixture just before serving. Garnish, if desired. Yield: 12 to 14 servings.

WHITE SANGRÍA FIZZ

carnation creations
welcome guests with flowers

wreath

materials
florist foam wreath • florist tape • florist wire
red carnations • ribbon

1 Soak florist foam wreath thoroughly in water; hang it over a sink or outdoors to drain excess water. Make a hanger by wrapping a piece of florist tape around foam several times. Place a piece of florist wire on top, and twist to form a hanging loop.

2 Cut flower stems 1½ inches below the blossom head, and push them into the form. Finish off with a loosely tied ribbon to conceal wire hanger. Carnations will last a week when kept moist, so add water to the foam every other day to prolong freshness. Place the arrangement in a sink, and slowly drizzle with water. Drain well before rehanging.

carnation pots

materials
florist foam sphere • red carnations • ceramic pots

1 Start with several shades of red carnations and choose ceramic pots in assorted sizes for containers. Place a moist florist foam sphere on each pot.

2 Cut flower stems about 2 inches below the blossom head, and push into the form to hug the surface. Begin with a ring of blooms around the rim of the pot; add flowers to fill in the remaining area. Each blossom should touch those next to it so the form is completely covered.

trade secrets

• Thoroughly soak florist foam before using. Add a packet of flower food to the water to increase the life of cut blooms. Many times this additive is included when flowers are purchased. If not, ask the florist for a small pouch or two.

• Spheres of florist foam come in assorted sizes. We used 2-inch, 4-inch, and 8-inch balls in our table arrangement. Circular forms also offer size options. When a foam wreath is filled with flowers and water, it becomes surprisingly heavy. Begin with a small product to understand the weight factor before trying to hang a large carnation wreath.

• If you're making a large wreath—12 inches around or more—wrap the form with chicken wire for added support (see photo above).

No-Fuss Dinner for Eight

NO MATTER HOW BUSY THE HOLIDAYS GET, YOU'RE NEVER TOO BUSY TO HAVE FRIENDS AND FAMILY OVER FOR A MEAL WITH THIS SIMPLE MENU. FOLLOW OUR SIMPLE PLAN AND YOU'LL HAVE A STRESS-FREE OPTION FOR YOUR NEXT GATHERING.

menu
serves 8

Herb-Roasted Pork Tenderloin • Roasted Garlic Mashed Potatoes
Easy Romaine Toss • Bakery rolls • Ambrosia Pie

HERB-ROASTED PORK TENDERLOIN

¼ cup soy sauce
¼ cup Worcestershire sauce
¼ cup vegetable oil
1 teaspoon dried thyme
1 teaspoon dried marjoram
1 teaspoon rubbed sage
1 teaspoon garlic powder
1 teaspoon onion powder
1 teaspoon ground ginger
1 teaspoon salt
1 teaspoon pepper
2 (1½-pound) packages pork tenderloins

Stir together first 11 ingredients in a shallow dish or heavy-duty zip-top plastic bag. Prick pork with a fork, and place in marinade, turning to coat. Cover or seal; let stand at room temperature 30 minutes, or chill 2 to 12 hours. Remove from marinade, discarding marinade. Place pork on a rack in a roasting pan.

Bake at 350° for 40 minutes or until a meat thermometer inserted into thickest portion registers 160°. Let pork stand 10 minutes before slicing. Yield: 8 servings.

ROASTED GARLIC MASHED POTATOES

There's no rule that says you have to peel potatoes for mashing. Scrub the skins well, and don't peel the potatoes for these crowd-pleasing mashers, and shave even more time off your game plan.

2 heads garlic, unpeeled*
Olive oil
2 pounds red potatoes, peeled and quartered
2 teaspoons salt, divided
¼ cup milk
¼ cup shredded Parmesan cheese
3 tablespoons butter or margarine
⅓ cup chopped fresh parsley
½ teaspoon pepper

Cut top off garlic, leaving heads intact. Place garlic heads on a piece of aluminum foil; drizzle with olive oil. Fold foil to seal.

Bake at 350° for 1 hour; cool 10 minutes. Remove outermost layers of papery skin from garlic. Squeeze out soft garlic pulp, and set aside.

Meanwhile, bring potatoes, 1 teaspoon salt, and water to cover to a boil in a Dutch oven; boil 15 to 20 minutes or until potatoes are tender. Drain well. Return potatoes to pan. Mash potatoes; stir in garlic, remaining 1 teaspoon salt, milk, and remaining ingredients. Mash until mixture is smooth. Yield: 8 servings.

*For an easy shortcut, substitute 2 tablespoons commercial roasted garlic in a jar for roasted garlic.

EASY ROMAINE TOSS

Blend this dressing ahead, and store it in the refrigerator to get a jump start on the salad.

⅓ cup sherry vinegar
¼ cup balsamic vinegar
2 teaspoons Dijon mustard
1 garlic clove, minced
½ teaspoon salt
¼ teaspoon coarsely ground pepper
½ cup walnut oil
½ cup olive oil
8 cups torn romaine lettuce or mixed salad greens
Toasted walnuts (optional)
Tomato wedges (optional)

Process first 6 ingredients in a blender or food processor until smooth. Turn blender on high; add oils in a slow, steady stream. Chill, if desired. Serve dressing at room temperature with lettuce and, if desired, toasted walnuts and tomato wedges. Yield: 8 servings.

Note: Substitute ½ cup olive oil for walnut oil.

AMBROSIA PIE

Holiday fruit blended with cream cheese and coconut makes a festive, make-ahead dessert.

1   (11-ounce) can mandarin oranges in light syrup
1   (8¼-ounce) can crushed pineapple in heavy syrup
1   (8-ounce) package cream cheese, softened
1   (14-ounce) can sweetened condensed milk
2½ cups frozen whipped topping, thawed and divided
¾   cup flaked coconut, toasted
1   (9-ounce) graham cracker crust (extra serving size)
Garnishes: maraschino cherries, pecan halves, additional toasted flaked coconut

Drain oranges and pineapple, reserving 2 tablespoons pineapple syrup. Gently press oranges and pineapple between layers of paper towels to remove excess moisture.

Beat cream cheese at medium-high speed with an electric mixer until creamy. Gradually add reserved pineapple syrup and milk, beating until smooth. Fold in 1½ cups whipped topping. Gently fold in orange-pineapple mixture and ¾ cup coconut. Spoon filling into crust. Cover; freeze until firm or up to 1 month.

Let pie stand at room temperature 20 minutes before serving. Dollop remaining 1 cup whipped topping on top of pie. Garnish, if desired. Yield: 1 (9-inch) pie.

AMBROSIA PIE

easy game plan

This simple meal will be ready in a snap with a little planning.

1 month ahead • Prepare and freeze the Ambrosia Pie.

1 week ahead • Prepare and chill the marinade for the pork and the salad vinaigrette up to a week before you serve it.

12 hours ahead • Marinate the pork tenderloins up to 12 hours before you roast them.

1 hour ahead • Prepare the mashed potatoes, and roast the pork.

just before serving • Warm some bakery-fresh yeast rolls, and toss the salad. Set the pie out as you serve dinner so it can soften.

CRANBERRY TAPENADE

SOURDOUGH-SAUSAGE
QUICHES

Appetizer Party

CAPTURE THE ESSENCE OF CHRISTMAS WITH THESE MOUTHWATERING MORSELS. THIS MENU PUTS A TWIST ON TRADITIONAL CHRISTMAS DINNER INGREDIENTS. HERE THEY APPEAR IN SERVING SIZES JUST RIGHT FOR A TASTING BUFFET.

menu
serves 12 to 16

Cranberry Tapenade • Sourdough-Sausage Quiches • Mini Turkey Sandwiches
Prosciutto-Wrapped Asparagus • Pumpkin Pie Biscotti • Maple-Pecan Tartlets
Cranberry-Pineapple Punch • Iced Eggnog

CRANBERRY TAPENADE

Purchased sweet potato chips make sturdy dippers for this festive relish.

1   small sweet potato (about 6 ounces)
1   small navel orange, unpeeled and quartered
2   cups fresh or frozen cranberries
½   cup sugar
2   jalapeño peppers, halved lengthwise and seeded
½   cup chopped pecans, toasted
3   tablespoons chopped fresh cilantro
⅛   teaspoon salt
⅛   teaspoon ground cinnamon
    Sweet potato chips
    Garnishes: whole fresh cranberries, fresh cilantro sprigs

Cook sweet potato in a small amount of boiling water just until barely tender. Drain and cool completely. Peel and finely dice sweet potato; set aside.

Position knife blade in food processor bowl; add orange quarters. Process until coarsely chopped, stopping to scrape down sides. Add 2 cups cranberries, sugar, and jalapeño pepper; pulse 2 or 3 times until mixture is finely chopped.

Transfer mixture to a bowl; stir in reserved sweet potato, pecans, and next 3 ingredients. Cover and chill at least 1 hour. Serve with sweet potato chips. Garnish, if desired. Yield: 2¼ cups.

SOURDOUGH-SAUSAGE QUICHES

These toasty little pastries laced with sage and sausage mimic the taste of turkey dressing.

2   (16-ounce) loaves sliced sourdough bread
⅓   cup butter or margarine, melted
¼   pound hot ground pork sausage
¼   cup minced celery
3   tablespoons minced onion
3   large eggs, lightly beaten
¾   cup half-and-half
½   cup (2 ounces) finely shredded mozzarella cheese
½   teaspoon poultry seasoning
¼   teaspoon salt
¼   teaspoon pepper
⅛   teaspoon rubbed sage
    Garnish: celery leaves

Cut bread slices into 40 rounds, using a 3-inch biscuit cutter. Roll each bread round lightly with a rolling pin. Brush both sides of each round lightly with melted butter. Press into miniature (1¾-inch) muffin pans lightly coated with cooking spray. Bake at 350° for 20 minutes or until crisp and golden.

Cook sausage, celery, and onion in a skillet over medium-high heat until sausage is browned, stirring until sausage is finely crumbled; drain.

Combine sausage mixture, eggs, and next 6 ingredients in a medium bowl; stir well. Spoon into prepared toast cups, filling three-fourths full.

Bake at 350° for 15 minutes or until set. Serve warm. Garnish, if desired. Yield: 40 appetizers.

TIP The key to any party-planning is to actually *have* a plan. Compile a list of everything you're going to serve and make a grocery list (including crackers, beverages, and paper goods). Remember to check off items as you go. Avoid preparing too many recipes. It's easier to multiply a few recipes than to juggle a bunch.

MINI TURKEY SANDWICHES

Favorite holiday flavors like turkey and cranberry sauce mingle in these bite-size delights.

- 1 (7- or 8-ounce) package small party rolls on aluminum tray
- ½ (3-ounce) package cream cheese, softened
- 2 tablespoons mayonnaise
- 2 tablespoons sour cream
- 1 tablespoon chutney
- ¼ teaspoon curry powder
- ¼ teaspoon ground red pepper
- ¼ pound very thinly sliced smoked turkey
- ½ cup whole-berry cranberry sauce
- 2 tablespoons minced onion

Remove rolls from aluminum tray. Slice rolls in half horizontally, using a serrated knife. Return bottom halves of rolls to tray.

Combine cream cheese, mayonnaise, and sour cream. Beat at low speed with an electric mixer until smooth. Stir in chutney, curry powder, and red pepper. Spread chutney mixture on cut sides of top halves of rolls. Set aside.

Place turkey on bottom halves of rolls. Combine cranberry sauce and onion; stir well. Spread cranberry mixture over turkey. Cover with tops of rolls. (You'll cut sandwiches apart after baking.)

Cover and bake at 350° for 20 to 30 minutes or until sandwiches are thoroughly heated. To serve, cut sandwiches apart with a sharp knife. Yield: 2 dozen.

PROSCIUTTO-WRAPPED ASPARAGUS

With just three ingredients, this simple, elegant appetizer delivers big-time flavor in small packages.

- 25 fresh asparagus spears (about 1½ pounds)
- About 1 tablespoon Dijon mustard
- 25 thin slices prosciutto or fully cooked ham (about ½ pound)

Snap off tough ends of asparagus. Cook asparagus in a small amount of boiling water 3 to 4 minutes. Drain, and plunge asparagus into ice water. Drain.

Spread about ⅛ teaspoon mustard on 1 side of each slice of prosciutto. Wrap prosciutto, mustard side in, around asparagus. Cover tightly, and chill up to 2 days. Yield: about 12 appetizer servings.

PUMPKIN PIE BISCOTTI

This twice-baked cookie recipe makes enough extras to package and send as gifts.

- 3½ cups all-purpose flour
- 1½ cups firmly packed brown sugar
- 2 teaspoons baking powder
- ½ teaspoon salt
- 2 teaspoons pumpkin pie spice
- ½ cup canned, mashed pumpkin
- 2 large eggs, lightly beaten
- 1 tablespoon vanilla extract
- 2 tablespoons butter or margarine
- 1¼ cups macadamia nuts, coarsely chopped

Combine first 5 ingredients in a large bowl; stir well. Combine pumpkin, eggs, and vanilla, stirring well with a wire whisk. Slowly add pumpkin mixture to flour mixture, stirring until dry ingredients are moistened. (Mixture will be very crumbly; it will gradually become moist after stirring.)

Melt butter in a large skillet over medium heat; add macadamia nuts. Cook, stirring constantly, until nuts are browned. Remove from heat, and cool completely. Knead or gently stir cooled nuts into dough.

Place dough on a lightly floured surface, and divide into 4 portions. Lightly flour hands, and shape each portion into a 15- x 1-inch log. Place logs 3 inches apart on lightly greased large cookie sheets.

Bake at 350° for 23 minutes; cool 15 minutes. Reduce oven temperature to 300°.

Cut each log crosswise into ½-inch slices, using a serrated knife. Place slices on ungreased baking sheets.

Bake at 300° for 15 minutes. Cool completely on wire racks. Yield: 8 dozen.

MINI TURKEY SANDWICHES

PUMPKIN PIE BISCOTTI

MAPLE-PECAN TARTLETS

109

MAPLE-PECAN TARTLETS

Ground cinnamon in the cream cheese pastry makes these petite pies something to write home about.

¾ cup firmly packed brown
  sugar
¼ cup maple syrup
1 tablespoon butter or margarine,
  melted
⅛ teaspoon salt
1 large egg, lightly beaten
¾ cup finely chopped pecans,
  toasted
  Cinnamon Pastry Shells

Beat first 5 ingredients in a small mixing bowl at medium speed with an electric mixer until blended. Stir in pecans. Spoon filling evenly into Cinnamon Pastry Shells.

Bake at 325° for 25 minutes or until set. Cool slightly. Remove from pans; cool completely on a wire rack. Yield: 2 dozen.

cinnamon pastry shells:

1 (3-ounce) package cream cheese,
  softened
⅓ cup butter or margarine, softened
1 cup all-purpose flour
¾ teaspoon ground cinnamon

Beat cream cheese and butter at medium speed with an electric mixer until creamy. Gradually add flour and cinnamon, beating at low speed just until ingredients are blended. Wrap dough in wax paper, and chill 2 hours.

Divide dough in half. Divide each half of dough into 12 balls. Place in lightly greased miniature (1¾-inch) muffin pans, shaping each into a shell. Yield: 2 dozen.

CRANBERRY-PINEAPPLE PUNCH

Look to our "Holiday How-To" box below for an ice fruit ring that will bring a festive addition to this punch. Use any cranberry fruit blend, like cran-raspberry or cran-cherry, for a twist on this crowd-pleaser.

1 (48-ounce) bottle cranberry juice
  drink
1 (48-ounce) can pineapple juice
½ cup sugar
2 teaspoons almond extract
1 (2-liter) bottle ginger ale, chilled

Stir together first 4 ingredients until sugar dissolves. Cover mixture; chill 8 hours.

Stir in ginger ale just before serving. Yield: 6½ quarts.

HOLIDAY HOW-TO

floating fruit ring
make it merry

Dress up a party with an icy fruit wreath in the punch bowl. You can use any flavor of juice to fill the ring to complement your punch.

materials
crushed ice • 6-cup ring mold • grapes, apple wedges, and orange slices • apple juice or water

1 Place 2 cups of crushed ice in a 6-cup ring mold. Lay 4 small clusters of seedless grapes over the ice.

2 Arrange apple wedges and 4 orange slices around grapes. Pour 2 cups apple juice or water around fruit almost to top of mold. Freeze 8 hours. To unmold, place mold in a large bowl of warm water for 5 seconds. Float wreath in punch bowl.

ICED EGGNOG

Here's a rich takeoff on iced coffee. Vanilla-rum ice cream cubes melt quickly to provide a punch of flavor.

3½ cups vanilla ice cream, softened
½ cup dark rum
2 quarts refrigerated eggnog
Freshly grated nutmeg

Combine softened ice cream and rum; stir until blended. Spoon mixture into ice cube trays. (You should be able to make about 28 ice-cream cubes.) Freeze at least 8 hours. (Ice-cream cubes will not freeze hard like ice. You'll be able to remove them as soft cubes.)

Fill individual glasses two-thirds full with eggnog. Add 2 or 3 ice-cream cubes to each glass. Sprinkle with nutmeg. Serve immediately. Yield: 8 cups.

Note: You can combine the eggnog and ice-cream cubes in a punch bowl and serve with a ladle, if desired.

Make-Ahead Buffet

HOST A LARGE GET-TOGETHER DURING THE HOLIDAY SEASON,
BUFFET-STYLE. GUESTS CAN MINGLE IN AN EASY ATMOSPHERE OF FESTIVE
HOSPITALITY AS THEY SERVE THEMSELVES.

menu
serves 10

Shrimp-and-Chicken Casserole • *Lemon-Almond Pilaf*
Roasted Red Pepper-and-Green Bean Salad • *Bakery rolls*
Two-Step Chocolate-Chip Pound Cake

SHRIMP-AND-CHICKEN CASSEROLE

No one will know this creamy dish overflowing with chicken, shrimp, and broccoli started with convenience products. It serves as a fitting center-piece to this make-ahead buffet, or bring it along to a covered-dish potluck.

4 cups water
1 pound unpeeled, medium-size fresh shrimp*
2 (16-ounce) packages frozen broccoli florets, thawed and well drained
1 (10¾-ounce) can cream of chicken soup, undiluted
1 (10¾-ounce) can cream of celery soup, undiluted
1 cup mayonnaise
3 tablespoons lemon juice
¼ teaspoon ground white pepper
4 cups chopped cooked chicken
1 cup (4 ounces) shredded Cheddar cheese
½ cup soft breadcrumbs
1 tablespoon butter or margarine, melted
¼ teaspoon paprika

Bring 4 cups water to a boil; add shrimp, and cook 3 to 5 minutes or just until shrimp turn pink. Drain and rinse with cold water. Peel shrimp, and devein, if desired. Set aside.

Spread broccoli evenly in a lightly greased 13- x 9-inch baking dish.

Stir together cream of chicken soup and next 4 ingredients until blended. Spread about one-third of mixture evenly over broccoli; top with chicken and shrimp. Spread remaining soup mixture evenly over chicken and shrimp. Cover and chill up to 8 hours.

Remove casserole from refrigerator, and let stand 30 minutes.

Bake, covered, at 350° for 30 minutes. Uncover and sprinkle with Cheddar cheese. Combine breadcrumbs and butter;

sprinkle over cheese, and bake 15 more minutes or until hot and bubbly. Sprinkle with paprika. Yield: 10 servings.

*You can substitute 1 (16-ounce) pack-age frozen ready-to-eat cooked shrimp for fresh shrimp. Thaw according to package directions, and remove tails, if necessary. Omit cooking.

Note: 1 (1½-pound) whole roasted chicken yields 4 cups chopped cooked chicken. To lighten this recipe, use light mayonnaise, fat-free cream of chicken and cream of celery soups, ¾ cup reduced-fat Cheddar cheese, and ¼ cup soft breadcrumbs.

LEMON-ALMOND PILAF

¾ cup sliced almonds
3 cups uncooked long-grain rice
3 tablespoons olive oil
3 (14½-ounce) cans chicken broth
1½ tablespoons grated lemon rind
3 tablespoons fresh lemon juice
⅓ cup minced fresh parsley
Garnish: fresh parsley sprigs

Cook almonds in a heavy Dutch oven over medium heat, stirring often, 4 to 5 minutes or until toasted. Remove almonds, and set aside.

Sauté rice in hot oil in Dutch oven, stirring often, 5 minutes or until golden.

Add broth, and bring to a boil. Cover, reduce heat, and simmer 18 minutes; remove rice mixture from heat, and let stand 5 minutes.

Stir in almonds, lemon rind, lemon juice, and minced parsley. Garnish, if desired. Yield: 10 servings.

Note: Cooked rice can be chilled 24 hours in the refrigerator. To reheat, microwave at HIGH 2 minutes; stir and microwave 2 more minutes. Stir in almonds, lemon rind, lemon juice, and minced parsley.

grocery list

staples on hand

¾ cup olive oil
6 tablespoons rice vinegar
2 teaspoons ground cumin
salt and ground black pepper
4 cups all-purpose flour
3 cups sugar
light corn syrup
2 teaspoons vanilla extract
1 cup mayonnaise
ground white pepper
paprika

general

¾ cup sliced almonds
3 cups long-grain rice
3 (14½-ounce) cans chicken broth
1 (15-ounce) jar roasted red bell peppers
1 (12-ounce) package semisweet chocolate morsels
1 (10¾-ounce) can cream of chicken soup
1 (10¾-ounce) can cream of celery soup
1 white bread slice (½ cup soft breadcrumbs)
2 dozen rolls

produce

1 bunch fresh parsley (⅓ cup chopped)
1 bunch fresh cilantro (½ cup chopped)
2 pounds fresh green beans
2 to 3 lemons

dairy

1¼ pounds butter
¾ cup milk
3 tablespoons half-and-half
6 large eggs
4 ounces Cheddar cheese

meat

1 pound medium-size shrimp
2 pounds bone-in chicken breasts or 1 (23-ounce) whole roasted chicken (4 cups chopped cooked)

frozen

2 (16-ounce) packages broccoli florets

buffet planner

a week or more before the party
• Buy all staples and ingredients for dishes to be made ahead.
• Buy or freeze plenty of ice cubes.
• Prepare and freeze Two-Step Chocolate-Chip Pound Cake without glaze.
• Plan the buffet centerpieces, if using any.
• Check all linens.

a few days before the party
• Do major housecleaning.

1 day before the party
• Toast almonds, and cook rice for Lemon-Almond Pilaf.
• Prepare Roasted Red Pepper-and-Green Bean Salad.
• Prepare Shrimp-and-Chicken Casserole, but do not bake. Cover and chill.
• Thaw pound cake, and drizzle with Fudgy Chocolate Glaze.
• Wash plates and glasses.
• Set up the buffet table and beverage service.

on the party day
• Give the house a light cleaning.
• Clear a space for your guests to leave coats.

1½ hours before party
• Let chicken casserole stand at room temperature 30 minutes; then bake.

15 minutes before party
• Reheat pilaf and rolls.

ROASTED RED PEPPER-AND-GREEN BEAN SALAD

2 pounds fresh green beans, trimmed
½ cup olive oil
6 tablespoons rice vinegar
2 teaspoons ground cumin
2 teaspoons freshly ground pepper
¾ teaspoon salt
½ cup chopped fresh cilantro
1 (15-ounce) jar roasted red bell peppers, drained and cut into strips

Arrange green beans in a steamer basket over boiling water. Cover and steam 10 minutes or until crisp-tender. Drain beans, and rinse with cold water.

Whisk together oil and next 5 ingredients in a large bowl until blended.

Add green beans and red peppers, tossing to coat. Cover salad, and chill 8 hours. Yield: 10 servings.

TWO-STEP CHOCOLATE-CHIP POUND CAKE

This cake requires a heavy-duty stand mixer with a 4-quart bowl and paddle attachment.

4 cups all-purpose flour
3 cups sugar
1 pound butter, softened
¾ cup milk
6 large eggs
2 teaspoons vanilla extract
1 cup (6 ounces) semisweet chocolate morsels
   Fudgy Chocolate Glaze

Place flour, sugar, butter, milk, eggs, and vanilla (in that order) in a 4-quart bowl. Beat at low speed with a heavy-duty mixer 1 minute, stopping to scrape down sides. Beat at medium speed 2 minutes. Stir in chocolate chips. Pour into a greased and floured 10-inch tube pan.

Bake at 325° for 1 hour and 30 minutes or until a wooden pick inserted in center comes out clean. Cool in pan on a wire rack 10 minutes. Remove cake from pan, and cool completely on a wire rack. Drizzle with Fudgy Chocolate Glaze. Yield: 1 (10-inch) cake.

Traditional Method: Beat butter at medium speed with an electric mixer 2 minutes or until creamy; gradually add sugar, beating until light and fluffy. Add eggs, 1 at a time, beating after each addition.

Add flour to butter mixture alternately with milk, beginning and ending with flour. Beat at low speed just until blended after each addition. Stir in chocolate morsels and vanilla. Pour batter into a greased and floured 10-inch tube pan. Bake as directed in two-step method. Drizzle with Fudgy Chocolate Glaze.

fudgy chocolate glaze:

1 cup (6 ounces) semisweet chocolate morsels
3 tablespoons butter or margarine
3 tablespoons half-and-half
1 tablespoon light corn syrup

Microwave all ingredients in a glass bowl at HIGH 1 minute; stir and microwave 1 more minute. Stir until smooth. Yield: 1 cup.

beverage basics

• If you're serving alcoholic beverages, allow one drink per hour per guest.
• One 750-milliliter bottle of wine contains 5 to 6 glasses of wine.
• If you're serving coffee, remember that a standard coffee cup holds 6 ounces, and a mug holds 10 to 12 ounces.
• Three quarts of iced tea serves 12.

TWO-STEP CHOCOLATE-CHIP POUND CAKE

Office Party Made Easy

SPREAD A LITTLE HOLIDAY CHEER AROUND YOUR OFFICE. HERE'S A SAMPLING OF TERRIFIC PORTABLE RECIPES THAT MAKE A PLEASING, FUSS-FREE MENU EVERYONE CAN ENJOY.

menu
serves 12 to 16

Mexican Cheese Ball • *Party Pinwheels* • *Spiced Holiday Pecans*
Festive Sandwich Wreath • *Cranberry-Caramel Bars*
Buttermilk Fudge Squares

MEXICAN CHEESE BALL

Taco seasoning and picante sauce give this cheese ball a spicy kick.

- ⅔ cup chopped pecans
- 1 tablespoon butter or margarine, melted
- ⅛ teaspoon salt
- 2 (8-ounce) packages cream cheese, softened
- 4 green onions, chopped
- ½ cup (2 ounces) shredded Cheddar cheese
- ¼ cup taco seasoning
- ¼ cup picante sauce
- Garnish: fresh parsley leaves

Bake pecans in a shallow pan at 275° for 20 to 30 minutes or until toasted, stirring occasionally. Stir in butter, and sprinkle with salt.

Stir together cream cheese and next 4 ingredients. Shape into a ball, and roll in toasted pecans. Cover and chill at least 2 hours. Garnish, if desired. Serve with breadsticks or assorted crackers. Yield: 4 cups.

PARTY PINWHEELS

These flavorful pinwheels will adapt to your schedule nicely. You can make them up to 24 hours in advance.

- 2 green onions
- 2 (8-ounce) packages cream cheese, softened
- 1 (1-ounce) envelope Ranch-style dressing mix
- 5 (12-inch) flour tortillas
- ¾ cup finely chopped pimiento-stuffed olives
- ¾ cup finely chopped ripe olives
- 1 (4.5-ounce) can chopped green chiles, drained
- 1 (4-ounce) jar diced pimiento, drained

Combine first 3 ingredients; spread evenly over 1 side of tortillas.

Combine olives, chiles, and pimiento; spread over cream cheese layer. Roll up tightly, jellyroll fashion. Wrap each roll in plastic wrap; chill at least 2 hours. To serve, remove plastic wrap, and cut each roll into 1-inch slices. Yield: 40 pinwheels.

SPICED HOLIDAY PECANS

Pecan halves get a toasting and a bit of spice, courtesy of cinnamon, red pepper, and hot sauce.

- 3 tablespoons butter or margarine, melted
- 3 tablespoons Worcestershire sauce
- 1 teaspoon salt
- ½ teaspoon ground red pepper
- ½ teaspoon ground cinnamon
- Dash of hot sauce
- 4 cups pecan halves

Stir together first 6 ingredients in a bowl. Add pecans, and toss gently to coat. Place in an ungreased 15- x 10-inch jelly-roll pan.

Bake at 300° for 25 to 28 minutes, stirring twice. Cool completely. Store in an airtight container. Yield: 4 cups.

TIP Use your favorite baskets lined with festive napkins or linens for transporting your food and displaying it attractively once you arrive.

MEXICAN CHEESE BALL

FESTIVE SANDWICH WREATH

FESTIVE SANDWICH WREATH

2   cups chopped cooked chicken
2   green onions, chopped
1   garlic clove
½   cup mayonnaise
½   teaspoon salt
¼   teaspoon pepper
20 party rye bread slices
20 party pumpernickel bread slices
    Garnishes: fresh parsley sprigs,
        chopped red bell pepper

Process first 6 ingredients in a food processor until combined, stopping to scrape down sides of processor. Spread rye bread slices evenly with chicken mixture, and top with pumpernickel slices. Arrange sandwiches vertically around a 9-inch serving dish, alternating rye and pumpernickel sides. Garnish, if desired. Yield: 20 appetizer servings.

CRANBERRY-CARAMEL BARS

1   cup fresh cranberries
2   tablespoons sugar
2   cups all-purpose flour
½   teaspoon baking soda
2   cups uncooked regular oats
½   cup sugar
½   cup firmly packed light brown sugar
1   cup butter or margarine, melted
1   (10-ounce) package chopped dates
¾   cup chopped pecans
1   (12-ounce) jar caramel sauce
⅓   cup all-purpose flour

Stir together cranberries and 2 tablespoons sugar in a small bowl; set aside.

Combine 2 cups flour and next 4 ingredients; stir in butter until mixture is crumbly. Reserve 1 cup flour mixture. Press remaining mixture into bottom of a lightly greased 13- x 9-inch baking dish.

Bake at 350° for 15 minutes. Sprinkle with dates, pecans, and cranberry mixture. Stir together caramel sauce and ⅓ cup flour; spoon over cranberries. Sprinkle with reserved 1 cup flour mixture. Bake 20 more minutes or until lightly browned. Cool on a wire rack. Cut into bars. Yield: 2 dozen.

BUTTERMILK FUDGE SQUARES

1 cup butter or margarine
1 cup water
¼ cup cocoa
½ cup buttermilk
2 large eggs
1 teaspoon baking soda
1 teaspoon vanilla extract
2 cups sugar
2 cups all-purpose flour
½ teaspoon salt
Chocolate-Buttermilk Frosting

Cook butter, 1 cup water, and cocoa in a small saucepan over low heat, stirring constantly, until butter melts and mixture is smooth; remove from heat.

Beat buttermilk and next 3 ingredients at medium speed with an electric mixer until smooth. Add butter mixture, beating until blended.

Combine sugar, flour, and salt; gradually add to buttermilk mixture, beating until blended. Pour into a greased 15- x 10-inch jellyroll pan.

Bake at 350° for 15 to 20 minutes or until cake is set. Spread Chocolate-Buttermilk Frosting over warm cake. Cut into squares while warm. Cool before serving. Yield: 2 dozen.

chocolate-buttermilk frosting:

1 cup butter or margarine
¼ cup cocoa
⅓ cup buttermilk
1 (16-ounce) package powdered sugar
1 teaspoon vanilla extract
¼ cup chopped pecans

Cook first 3 ingredients in a medium saucepan over medium heat, stirring constantly, until butter melts and mixture is smooth. Remove from heat; stir in powdered sugar, vanilla, and pecans. Yield: about 2½ cups.

more quick crowd-pleasing recipes

pesto dip Combine 1 (3.4-ounce) jar pesto sauce, 1 (8-ounce) container sour cream, and ⅓ cup chopped dried tomatoes in oil. Serve with vegetables. Yield: 1½ cups.

fruit dip Combine 1 (8-ounce) container sour cream, 1 tablespoon sugar, ½ teaspoon pumpkin pie spice, and 1 teaspoon vanilla extract. Serve with fruit. Yield: 1 cup.

easy guacamole Combine 1 ripe avocado, peeled and mashed; 2 tablespoons picante sauce; ¾ teaspoon lime juice; and ¼ teaspoon garlic salt. Serve with tortilla chips. Yield: 1 cup.

wine punch Stir together 1 (3-liter) bottle rosé and 1 (12-ounce) can frozen lemonade concentrate, thawed and undiluted; add 1 (2-liter) bottle lemon-lime soft drink just before serving. Serve over ice. Yield: 5½ quarts.

cranberry fruit punch Stir together 1 (48-ounce) bottle cranberry juice cocktail and 1 (46-ounce) can pink grapefruit juice; add 1 (1-liter) bottle ginger ale just before serving. Serve over ice. Yield: 1 gallon.

BUTTERMILK FUDGE SQUARES

MOCHA CHIFFON CAKE

Holiday Dessert Party

TASTY CONFECTIONS AWAIT AT THIS GRACIOUS GALA.
FROM SIMPLE POUND CAKE AND BUTTER COOKIES TO FANCY CHAMPAGNE
SABAYON, THERE'S A DESSERT FOR EVERYONE.

menu
serves 12 to 15

Mocha Chiffon Cake • *Gentleman's Pound Cake*
Honey-Pecan Tart • *Butter Cookies* • *Smoky Mountain Snowcaps*
Champagne Sabayon • *Champagne* • *Coffee*

MOCHA CHIFFON CAKE

- ¾ cup boiling water
- ½ cup cocoa
- 1 teaspoon instant coffee granules
- 1¾ cups cake flour
- 1¾ cups sugar
- 1½ teaspoons baking soda
- ½ teaspoon salt
- 8 large eggs, separated
- ½ cup vegetable oil
- 2 teaspoons vanilla extract
- ½ teaspoon cream of tartar
- Chocolate-Coffee Buttercream Filling
- Chocolate Fudge Frosting
- Garnish: chocolate-covered coffee beans

Stir together first 3 ingredients until blended; cool.

Combine flour and next 3 ingredients in a large mixing bowl. Add cocoa mixture, egg yolks, oil, and vanilla; beat at medium speed with an electric mixer until smooth.

Beat egg whites and cream of tartar at high speed with an electric mixer until foamy. Fold into batter. Pour batter into 4 greased and floured 9-inch round cakepans.

Bake, 2 layers at a time, at 325° for 17 to 20 minutes or until a wooden pick inserted in center comes out clean. Cool in pans on wire racks 10 minutes. Remove from pans, and cool on wire racks covered with plastic wrap or wax paper to prevent layers from adhering to racks.

Spread about ½ cup Chocolate-Coffee Buttercream Filling between layers. Frost with Chocolate Fudge Frosting. Garnish, if desired. Store in refrigerator. Yield: 1 (9-inch) layer cake.

chocolate-coffee buttercream filling:

- ⅔ cup butter, softened
- 2½ cups powdered sugar
- 1 tablespoon cocoa
- ½ cup whipping cream
- 2 teaspoons instant coffee granules
- 2 teaspoons coffee liqueur

Beat first 3 ingredients at medium speed with an electric mixer until fluffy.

Microwave whipping cream at MEDIUM (50% power) until warm (do not boil). Stir together warm cream and coffee granules until dissolved; cool. Add whipping cream mixture and liqueur to butter mixture, beating until smooth. Yield: 1¾ cups.

Note: Substitute 1 teaspoon vanilla extract for liqueur.

chocolate fudge frosting:

- 1 cup butter, softened
- ⅓ cup cocoa
- 6 cups powdered sugar
- ⅓ cup milk

Beat butter at medium speed with an electric mixer until creamy. Add cocoa and remaining ingredients, beating until smooth. Yield: 3½ cups.

Note: To a make a torte, cut each cake layer in half horizontally with a serrated knife, and use ¼ cup Chocolate-Coffee Buttercream Filling between layers. Frost as directed.

GENTLEMAN'S POUND CAKE

Ladies and gentlemen alike will indulge in this bourbon-soaked pound cake. Get a jump start on your dessert party, and make it up to a week ahead.

    2   cups butter or margarine,
        softened
    3   cups sugar, divided
    8   large eggs, separated
    1   cup bourbon, divided
  2½   teaspoons vanilla extract
    3   cups all-purpose flour
    ¾   cup chopped pecans, toasted
        Powdered sugar

Beat butter and 2 cups sugar at medium speed with an electric mixer 5 to 7 minutes. Add egg yolks, 1 at a time, beating just until yellow disappears.

Stir together ½ cup bourbon and vanilla. Add flour to butter mixture alternately with bourbon mixture, beginning and ending with flour. Beat at low speed just until blended after each addition.

Beat egg whites at high speed with an electric mixer until foamy. Add remaining 1 cup sugar, 1 tablespoon at a time, beating until stiff peaks form and sugar dissolves (2 to 4 minutes). Fold into cake batter.

Sprinkle half of pecans into a greased and floured 10-inch tube pan. Fold remaining pecans into cake batter, and pour into pan.

Bake at 350° for 1 hour and 25 minutes or until a long wooden pick inserted in center comes out clean. Cool cake in pan on a wire rack 10 to 15 minutes; remove cake from pan, and cool on wire rack.

Moisten several layers of cheesecloth with remaining ½ cup bourbon; cover cake completely with cheesecloth. Place in an airtight container, and store in a cool place 1 week, remoistening cheesecloth as needed. Sprinkle with powdered sugar just before serving. Yield: 1 (10-inch) cake.

HONEY-PECAN TART

A drizzle of melted bittersweet chocolate complements the richness of this holiday favorite.

    1   cup sugar
    ¼   cup water
    1   cup whipping cream
    ¼   cup unsalted butter, cut into small
        pieces
    ¼   cup honey
    ½   teaspoon salt
  2½   cups pecan halves, coarsely
        chopped
    1   (15-ounce) package refrigerated
        piecrusts
    2   teaspoons sugar, divided
    ½   (4-ounce) package bittersweet
        chocolate, chopped

Bring 1 cup sugar and ¼ cup water to a boil in a medium-size heavy saucepan, stirring until sugar dissolves. Cover and boil over medium-high heat, without stirring, 8 minutes or until golden, swirling pan occasionally.

Remove from heat, and gradually stir in whipping cream (mixture will bubble with addition of cream).

Add butter, honey, and salt, stirring until smooth. Stir in pecans, and simmer over medium heat, stirring occasionally, 5 minutes. Remove from heat, and cool completely.

Unfold 1 piecrust on a lightly floured surface, and roll into an 11-inch circle. Fit into a 9-inch tart pan with removable bottom. Trim edges. Freeze crust 30 minutes.

Spread pecan mixture into crust. Unfold remaining piecrust, and roll into a 10-inch circle. Place over mixture, pressing into bottom crust to seal; trim edges. Sprinkle with 1 teaspoon sugar. Freeze 30 minutes.

Bake at 400° for 30 minutes. Cool on a wire rack.

Place chocolate in a small heavy-duty zip-top plastic bag; seal. Submerge in hot water until chocolate melts. Snip a tiny hole in 1 corner of bag, and drizzle chocolate over tart. Sprinkle with remaining 1 teaspoon sugar. Yield: 1 (9-inch) tart.

BUTTER COOKIES

We recommend using real butter for the ultimate, melt-in-your-mouth result.

  1½   cups butter, softened
  1¼   cups sugar
    1   large egg
    1   teaspoon vanilla extract
    2   cups all-purpose flour
    ¾   cup strawberry preserves

Beat butter and sugar at medium speed with an electric mixer until fluffy. Add egg and vanilla, beating well. Add flour, beating just until mixture is blended.

Divide dough into 3 portions; roll each portion on wax paper into a 12-inch log. Cover and chill 8 hours.

Cut each log into ½-inch-thick slices; place on lightly greased baking sheets. Press thumb in center of each slice to make an indentation; fill with ½ teaspoon preserves.

Bake at 350° for 10 minutes or until edges are lightly browned. Remove to wire racks to cool. Freeze, if desired. Yield: 6 dozen.

SMOKY MOUNTAIN SNOWCAPS

    6   ounces white chocolate,
        chopped
    ¾   cup butter or margarine,
        softened
    1   cup sugar
    3   large eggs
    1   teaspoon vanilla extract
  3½   cups all-purpose flour
    1   teaspoon baking powder
    ¾   teaspoon salt
    ⅛   teaspoon ground nutmeg
  1½   cups chopped walnuts, toasted
    ½   cup powdered sugar

Melt white chocolate in a small saucepan over low heat, stirring until chocolate is smooth.

Beat butter and 1 cup sugar at medium speed with an electric mixer 5 minutes or until fluffy. Add eggs, 1 at a time, beating until blended. Add vanilla, beating well. Add melted chocolate, and beat 30 seconds.

Combine flour and next 3 ingredients; add to butter mixture, beating until blended. Stir in walnuts. Drop dough by heaping tablespoonfuls onto lightly greased baking sheets.

Bake at 350° for 10 to 12 minutes or until edges are lightly browned. Remove to wire racks to cool completely. Sprinkle with powdered sugar. Freeze, if desired. Yield: 3½ dozen.

CHAMPAGNE SABAYON

   8   egg yolks
 ⅔   cup sugar
1½   cups champagne
   1   pint each of fresh raspberries, blueberries, and strawberries

Whisk together egg yolks and sugar in a heavy saucepan over low heat until blended. Whisk in champagne; cook, whisking constantly, 10 minutes or until mixture reaches 160° and is thickened. Chill, if desired.

Spoon champagne mixture over fresh berries. Yield: 12 servings.

CHAMPAGNE SABAYON, GENTLEMAN'S POUND CAKE, AND BUTTER COOKIES

Our Favorite Holiday Feast

THE AROMAS OF TURKEY, PORK LOIN, DRESSING, AND SWEET POTATOES ANNOUNCE SOME OF OUR FOODS STAFF'S FAVORITE HOLIDAY RECIPES IN ONE MAGNIFICENT MEAL.

menu
serves 8

Orange-Dijon Pork Loin or Maple-Plum Glazed Turkey Breast • *Cornbread Dressing*
Roasted Root Vegetables • *Garlic Green Beans* • *Sweet Onion Pudding*
Crescent Rolls or Butter Muffins • *Caramel-Applesauce Cobbler with Bourbon-Pecan Ice Cream*

ORANGE-DIJON PORK LOIN

  2 teaspoons dried thyme
  1 teaspoon salt
  1 teaspoon rubbed sage
  ¼ teaspoon ground allspice
  ¼ teaspoon pepper
  1 (4- to 5-pound) rolled boneless
     pork loin roast
     Orange-Dijon Sauce

Combine first 5 ingredients; rub mixture evenly over roast. Place roast in a lightly greased 13- x 9-inch pan.

Bake at 325° for 1 hour. Cover and bake 30 more minutes or until a meat thermometer inserted into thickest portion registers 160°. Top with Orange-Dijon Sauce. Yield: 8 servings.

orange-dijon sauce:

  2 (12-ounce) jars orange marmalade
  ¼ cup Dijon mustard
  ¼ cup Worcestershire sauce
  1 teaspoon ground ginger
  4 large garlic cloves, minced

Bring all ingredients to a boil in a small saucepan over medium heat. Serve with pork loin. Yield: 2 cups.

MAPLE-PLUM GLAZED TURKEY BREAST

Let the turkey stand 20 minutes before carving to allow the juices to be reabsorbed.

  2 cups red plum jam
  1 cup maple syrup
  ¼ cup cider vinegar
  1 tablespoon grated lemon rind
  2 tablespoons fresh lemon juice
  1 teaspoon dry mustard
  1 (5- to 5½-pound) bone-in turkey
     breast
  ½ teaspoon salt
  8 fresh sage sprigs

Bring first 6 ingredients to a boil in a large saucepan over medium-high heat; reduce heat to medium-low, and cook, stirring often, 25 minutes or until thickened and bubbly. Remove from heat; cool completely.

Reserve 1½ cups sauce; cover and chill. Set aside remaining maple-plum sauce for basting.

Using fingers, carefully loosen skin from turkey without totally detaching skin; sprinkle salt evenly under skin, and carefully place 4 sage sprigs on each side of breast. Replace skin. Place turkey in a lightly greased 11- x 7-inch baking dish.

Spread ¾ cup maple-plum sauce evenly over turkey; cover loosely with aluminum foil.

Bake at 325° for 1 hour; uncover and bake 1 more hour or until a meat thermometer registers 170°, basting with remaining ¾ cup maple-plum sauce every 15 minutes.

Remove turkey from baking dish; cool. Wrap in plastic wrap, then aluminum foil; chill 8 hours. Serve at room temperature.

Cook reserved 1½ cups maple-plum sauce until thoroughly heated; serve with turkey. Yield: 10 servings.

Maple-Plum Glazed Turkey Tenderloins: Substitute 2 (16-ounce) packages turkey tenderloins for breast, if desired. Place tenderloins on a rack in a broiler pan coated with cooking spray; sprinkle evenly with salt, omitting sage. Baste evenly with ¾ cup maple-plum sauce. Bake at 425° for 25 to 30 minutes or until done, basting often with remaining ¾ cup maple-plum sauce.

ORANGE-DIJON PORK LOIN, ROASTED ROOT VEGETABLES,
GARLIC GREEN BEANS, AND BUTTER MUFFINS

...AD DRESSING

...s a Southern classic.
...roast or turkey.

....ups cornmeal
½ cup all-purpose flour
2 teaspoons baking powder
1 teaspoon baking soda
1 teaspoon salt
1 teaspoon sugar (optional)
6 large eggs, divided
2 cups buttermilk
2 tablespoons bacon drippings or
   melted butter
½ cup butter or margarine
3 bunches green onions, chopped
4 celery ribs, chopped
1 (16-ounce) package herb-
   seasoned stuffing mix
5 (14½-ounce) cans chicken
   broth

Combine first 5 ingredients and, if desired, sugar in a large bowl.

Stir together 2 eggs and buttermilk; add to dry ingredients, stirring just until moistened.

Heat bacon drippings in a 10-inch cast-iron skillet or 9-inch round cakepan in oven at 425° for 5 minutes. Stir hot drippings into batter. Pour batter into hot skillet.

Bake at 425° for 25 minutes or until golden; cool and crumble. Freeze in a large heavy-duty zip-top plastic bag up to 1 month, if desired. Thaw in refrigerator.

Melt ½ cup butter in a large skillet over medium heat; add green onions and celery, and sauté until tender.

Stir together remaining 4 eggs in a large bowl; stir in cornbread, green onions mixture, stuffing mix, and chicken broth until blended.

Spoon dressing into a lightly greased 13- x 9-inch baking dish and a lightly greased 9-inch square baking dish. Cover dressing, and freeze up to 3 months, if desired; thaw in refrigerator 8 hours.

Bake 13- x 9-inch dish, uncovered, at 350° for 1 hour or until lightly browned. Bake 9-inch square dish, uncovered, at 350° for 50 minutes or until lightly browned. Yield: 12 servings.

ROASTED ROOT VEGETABLES

The combination of colors and flavors in these vegetables will delight your family. It's sure to become a holiday mealtime tradition.

1 (1-pound) bag parsnips
6 large turnips
2 large sweet potatoes
1 large rutabaga
6 large beets
   Vegetable cooking spray
1 teaspoon salt, divided
1 teaspoon pepper, divided
2 tablespoons butter or margarine,
   melted

Peel first 5 ingredients, and cut into large pieces. Coat 2 aluminum foil-lined baking sheets with cooking spray.

Arrange parsnip, turnip, sweet potato, and rutabaga on a baking sheet. Lightly coat vegetables with cooking spray, and sprinkle with ¾ teaspoon salt and ¾ teaspoon pepper.

Arrange beets on remaining baking sheet; lightly coat with cooking spray, and sprinkle with remaining ¼ teaspoon salt and ¼ teaspoon pepper.

Bake vegetables at 425°, stirring occasionally, 35 to 45 minutes or until tender. (Pans may need to be rearranged after 15 to 20 minutes to ensure even cooking.)

Toss vegetables with melted butter. Yield: 8 servings.

Note: We cooked the beets separately to keep them from bleeding into the other vegetables.

CORNBREAD DRESSING

GARLIC GREEN BEANS

    2 pounds fresh green beans,
       trimmed
    1 cup boiling water
    1 teaspoon salt
  ¼ cup butter or margarine
    4 garlic cloves, pressed
  ¼ teaspoon lemon pepper
  ¼ cup chopped fresh parsley

Place first 3 ingredients in a Dutch oven; cover and cook over medium heat 30 minutes. Drain.

Melt butter in Dutch oven; add garlic and lemon pepper, and sauté mixture over medium heat 1 to 2 minutes.

Add green beans; sauté 5 minutes. Sprinkle with parsley. Yield: 8 servings.

SWEET ONION PUDDING

Simple ingredients blend for a decadent savory pudding.

    2 cups whipping cream
    1 (3-ounce) package shredded
       Parmesan cheese
    6 large eggs, lightly beaten
    3 tablespoons all-purpose flour
    2 tablespoons sugar
    2 teaspoons baking powder
    1 teaspoon salt
  ½ cup butter or margarine
    6 medium-size sweet onions, thinly
       sliced

Stir together first 3 ingredients in a large bowl. Combine flour and next 3 ingredients; gradually stir into egg mixture. Set aside.

Melt butter in a large skillet over medium heat; add onion. Cook, stirring often, 30 to 40 minutes or until caramel colored. Remove onion from heat.

Stir onion into egg mixture; spoon into a lightly greased 13- x 9-inch baking dish. Bake at 350° for 30 minutes or until set. Yield: 8 servings.

CRESCENT ROLLS

Using rapid-rise yeast cuts the rising time considerably for these tender, buttery rolls.

    1 (¼-ounce) envelope rapid-rise
       yeast
    1 teaspoon sugar
  ¼ cup warm water (100° to 110°)
  ½ cup shortening or butter,
       melted
  ¼ cup sugar
    2 large eggs, lightly beaten
    1 cup warm water (100° to 110°)
    1 teaspoon salt
4½ to 4¾ cups all-purpose flour,
       divided
  ¼ cup butter, melted

Combine yeast, 1 teaspoon sugar, and ¼ cup warm water in a 1-cup liquid measuring cup, and let stand 5 minutes.

Combine yeast mixture, shortening, and next 4 ingredients in a large mixing bowl; stir in 2 cups flour. Beat at medium speed with an electric mixer 1 minute. Gradually stir in enough remaining flour to make a soft dough.

Turn dough out onto a floured surface, and knead until smooth and elastic (about 5 minutes). Place in a well-greased bowl, turning to grease top. Cover and let rise in a warm place (85°), free from drafts, 45 minutes, or until doubled in bulk.

Punch dough down, and divide into fourths. Roll each portion into an 11-inch circle. Cut each circle into 8 wedges; roll up each wedge, beginning at wide end. Place on lightly greased baking sheets, point sides down, and curve slightly. Brush with ¼ cup melted butter. Cover and let rise in a warm place, free from drafts, 20 minutes or until doubled in bulk.

Bake at 375° for 10 to 12 minutes. Yield: 32 rolls.

tablesetting secrets

• If you don't have elegant china and crystal, you can still go formal. Dress your table with sparkle—a piece of gold fabric or a gauzy silver overlay on top of a white tablecloth is a great way to begin. Or purchase metallic gold and silver star-shaped confetti to scatter down the table as a runner.

• Long-stemmed roses have large flower heads, so just a few can create a dynamic arrangement. Spray roses are smaller, with each stem supporting multiple blooms. Choose the correct-size flower for your container, and consider mixing the two types for an interesting combination.

• Avoid using highly fragrant flowers in your centerpieces. Their sweetness engages in an unpleasant duel with food aromas. Some major offenders include lilies, paperwhites, and hyacinths.

• Tie glittery ribbon around the base of an everyday water goblet, and slip a small fresh flower into the knot.

• Personalize your inexpensive linen napkins with a handmade monogram or decorative edge. Paint pens present unlimited possibilities.

• Use lots of candles, and turn down the lights.

dance of the silverware

• Your menu helps determine the place setting with the flatware laid out in order of use. If salad is a separate course, that fork is placed on the left, first in line. The dinner fork comes next, residing beside the plate.

• Place the bread plate above the forks. Arrange the butter knife across the top of the bread plate, handle to the right, blade facing downward. The napkin rests to the left of the forks with the folded edge toward the right. A more elaborately folded napkin may be centered on the dinner plate.

• On the place setting's right side, align the dinner knife next to the plate, the blade facing inward. When the menu calls for soup, the appropriate spoon resides to the right of the dinner knife. Above this arrangement, locate your glassware. Water glasses are situated closest to the plate with the wine goblet following closely to the right.

• Dessert utensils may be handled one of two ways. The appropriate spoon or fork may be placed horizontally above the dinner plate or served on the saucer with dessert.

BUTTER MUFFINS

These bite-size quick breads will melt in your mouth.

2 cups self-rising flour
1 (8-ounce) container sour cream
1 cup butter or margarine, melted

Stir together all ingredients just until blended.

Spoon batter into lightly greased miniature (1¾-inch) muffin pans, filling to the top.

Bake at 350° for 25 minutes or until lightly browned. Yield: 2½ dozen.

CARAMEL-APPLESAUCE COBBLER WITH BOURBON-PECAN ICE CREAM

This spruced-up cobbler is a nice alternative to apple pie. Store-bought piecrusts make preparation easy, and bourbon-spiked ice cream crowns the dessert for a dazzling finish.

½ cup butter or margarine
12 large Granny Smith apples, peeled and sliced
2 cups sugar
2 tablespoons lemon juice
1 (15-ounce) package refrigerated piecrusts
Bourbon-Pecan Ice Cream

Melt butter in a large Dutch oven over medium-high heat. Add apple, sugar, and lemon juice; cook, stirring often, 20 to 25 minutes or until apple is caramel-colored.

Spoon into a shallow, greased 2-quart baking dish.

Roll each piecrust to press out fold lines; cut into ½-inch strips.

Arrange strips in a lattice design over filling; fold edges under. Place remaining strips on a baking sheet.

Bake remaining strips at 425° for 8 to 10 minutes or until golden. Set aside to serve with cobbler.

Bake cobbler at 425° for 20 to 25 minutes or until crust is golden.

Serve cobbler warm with pastry strips and Bourbon-Pecan Ice Cream. Yield: 8 servings.

bourbon-pecan ice cream:

2 pints homemade-style vanilla ice cream, softened (we tested with Blue Bell)
1 cup chopped pecans, toasted
¼ cup bourbon

Stir together all ingredients; freeze 4 hours. Yield: 2 pints.

CARAMEL-APPLESAUCE COBBLER WITH
BOURBON-PECAN ICE CREAM

A Traditional Christmas Dinner

CHRISTMAS DINNER IN THE SOUTH IS ALL ABOUT RELISHING UNINTERRUPTED FAMILY TIME AROUND THE TABLE. MAY THIS FEAST—COMPLETE WITH LOVING TABLETOP TOUCHES AND A FOOLPROOF PLAN—INSPIRE YOU TO EXPERIENCE THE DAY TO THE FULLEST.

menu
serves 8

Roast Turkey with Thyme Butter and Shallots

Last-Minute Gravy • *Rustic Corn Dressing* • *Apple Salad* • *Walnut Cranberry Sauce*

Roasted and Smashed Sweet Potatoes • *Gratin of Broccoli in Béchamel* • *Shredded Brussels Sprouts*

Deep-Dish Pecan Pie • *Cheesecake Flan*

ROAST TURKEY WITH THYME BUTTER AND SHALLOTS

If you're diligent about basting this bird near the end of roasting, you'll end up with moist, golden results.

1   (14-pound) turkey
Salt and freshly ground pepper
¾ cup unsalted butter, softened
2   tablespoons chopped fresh thyme
12 large shallots
2   tablespoons olive oil
Garnish: fresh thyme sprigs

If you buy a frozen bird, remember to allow at least 3 days for it to thaw in the refrigerator.

Remove giblets and neck from turkey; reserve for making homemade broth, if desired. Rinse turkey with cold water; pat dry. Sprinkle cavity with salt and pepper. Place turkey, breast side up, in a greased broiler pan.

Combine softened butter and 2 tablespoons chopped thyme, stirring well.

Using fingers, carefully loosen skin from turkey at neck area, working down to breast and thigh area. Spread ¼ cup butter mixture under skin.

Tie legs together with heavy string, or tuck them under flap of skin. Lift wingtips up and over back, and tuck under bird. Generously rub salt and pepper over turkey. Tent turkey loosely with aluminum foil; roast at 325° for 1 hour.

Melt remaining thyme butter in a small saucepan over low heat; set aside for basting.

Peel shallots and place in a bowl; drizzle with olive oil, and sprinkle generously with salt and pepper. Set aside.

Uncover turkey; baste with several tablespoons melted thyme butter mixture. Roast 1 hour, basting occasionally with butter mixture. After second hour of roasting, scatter shallots in pan around turkey; baste turkey. Roast 1 more hour or until a meat thermometer inserted into meaty part of thigh registers 180°, basting turkey and shallots every 15 minutes with butter mixture and pan drippings.

When turkey is done, carefully transfer to a serving platter; arrange shallots around turkey. Cover with foil; let turkey rest 15 minutes before carving. Reserve drippings in pan for Last-Minute Gravy. Prepare gravy. Garnish platter just before serving, if desired. Yield: 14 servings.

---

tablesetting tips

It's fairly easy to add a theme or color scheme to your holiday table. Pull out your favorite serving pieces, old and new china, holiday place mats, candles, napkins, and napkin rings. Most likely there will be a common thread among your collection; it might be color, pattern, shape, or texture. Before you know it, you'll be mixing and matching elements for a beautifully original table.

LAST-MINUTE GRAVY

Don't clean your broiler pan before making gravy. That's where all the goodness is. We suggest whisking the gravy right in the same pan while the roasted turkey rests on a platter.

½ cup reserved pan drippings
½ cup all-purpose flour
1½ cups apple cider
1½ cups turkey or chicken broth
¾ teaspoon salt
¾ teaspoon freshly ground pepper

Set broiler pan over 2 burners. Whisk flour into drippings in pan. Cook over medium heat until flour mixture (roux) is dark golden, stirring constantly to loosen any browned bits from bottom of pan. Gradually add cider and broth; cook, stirring constantly, 5 to 10 minutes or until gravy is thickened. Stir in salt and pepper. Yield: 3 cups.

sipping selections

• Pinot Noir is an all-purpose, affordable red wine. It's an excellent selection for this Christmas menu. A medium-bodied Chardonnay provides a popular white wine option that will complement roast turkey and all the trimmings. Serve Chardonnay well chilled and Pinot Noir lightly chilled or at room temperature.
• To choose wine that pleases you, just read the back label of a wine bottle for a description of its particular characteristics.
• For the children, try serving Cranapple juice, apple juice, or sparkling Catawba.

RUSTIC CORN DRESSING

Smoked bacon and roasted corn make this dressing unique.

1 (29-ounce) can whole kernel corn, drained (2¾ cups)
1 pound smoked bacon (we tested with Nueske's)
2 cups chopped onion
1½ cups chopped celery
4 garlic cloves, chopped
½ cup butter or margarine, melted
6 cups (12 ounces) stuffing (we tested with Pepperidge Farm cubed country-style stuffing)
1½ cups coarsely chopped pecans, toasted
1 large egg, lightly beaten
2 to 2¾ cups chicken or turkey broth
½ teaspoon salt
1 teaspoon freshly ground pepper

Press corn between several layers of paper towels to remove excess moisture. Set aside.

Cook bacon in a large skillet over medium heat until crisp; remove bacon, reserving 2 tablespoons drippings in skillet. Crumble bacon; set aside. Add corn to skillet; toss to coat. Cook over high heat, stirring constantly, until corn is roasted in appearance. Transfer corn to a large bowl.

Cook onion, celery, and garlic in butter in large skillet over medium-high heat, stirring constantly, until tender. Transfer to large bowl. Add stuffing, crumbled bacon, and pecans, stirring well. Add egg, desired amount of broth, salt, and pepper to stuffing mixture; stir gently.

Spoon dressing into a lightly greased 13- x 9-inch pan. Bake, uncovered, at 325° for 1 hour or until well browned. Yield: 10 servings.

APPLE SALAD

We recommend Fuji, Braeburn, or Gala apples for this simple salad because of their crisp texture. Give it time to chill before serving.

5 to 6 apples, chopped (8 cups)
4 celery ribs, chopped (2 cups)
1 cup coarsely chopped pecans
1 cup chopped pitted dates
1 cup mayonnaise
2 tablespoons sugar
2 tablespoons milk

Combine first 4 ingredients in a large bowl; toss well.

Combine mayonnaise, sugar, and milk, stirring until blended. Add mayonnaise mixture to apple mixture, tossing to coat. Cover and chill. Yield: 12 cups.

WALNUT CRANBERRY SAUCE

A hint of cinnamon, splash of dark vinegar, and handful of toasted nuts makes this cranberry sauce worthy of gift giving. Deliver it in a jar tied with ribbon.

1 (16-ounce) can whole-berry cranberry sauce
⅓ cup strawberry preserves
1½ tablespoons sugar
¼ teaspoon ground cinnamon
½ cup coarsely chopped walnuts, toasted
1 tablespoon balsamic vinegar or red wine such as Pinot Noir

Combine first 4 ingredients in a saucepan. Cook over medium heat, stirring often, just until thoroughly heated. Remove from heat; stir in walnuts and vinegar. Cover and chill until ready to serve. Serve with turkey or ham. Yield: 2¼ cups.

ROASTED AND SMASHED SWEET POTATOES

These sweet potatoes get caramelized during roasting, so when you mash them, a wonderful rich and sweet flavor comes forth. A small dollop makes the perfect serving.

    3   pounds sweet potatoes, peeled and
        cut into 1½-inch chunks
    3   tablespoons olive oil
    ¾   teaspoon salt
    ½   teaspoon freshly ground pepper
    ¼   cup butter or margarine, cut into
        pieces
    ⅔   cup half-and-half, heated
    ¼   cup firmly packed light brown sugar

Place sweet potato chunks in a large greased roasting pan; drizzle with olive oil. Sprinkle with salt and pepper; toss well. Spread sweet potato chunks in a single layer. Roast at 400° for 30 to 40 minutes or until sweet potatoes are very tender and roasted in appearance, stirring occasionally.

Transfer roasted sweet potatoes to a large bowl while still warm; add butter and mash with a potato masher. Add half-and-half and brown sugar; mash until fluffy. Serve warm. Yield: 8 servings.

Make-Ahead: Transfer roasted sweet potatoes to a Dutch oven or large saucepan; add butter and mash. Cover and chill overnight. Before serving, let sweet potato mixture stand at room temperature about 30 minutes. Add half-and-half and brown sugar; cook over low heat until thoroughly heated, mashing until fluffy.

turkey basics
tips for success and safety

• Thaw turkey, breast side up, in its unopened wrapper on a tray in the refrigerator. (Thawing at room temperature allows bacterial growth.) Allow at least one day of thawing for every 4 pounds.

• Short on time? Don't panic. Check the wrapper to make sure it's not torn. (Use another plastic bag if it is.) Place turkey, breast side down, in its unopened wrapper in a container; cover turkey with cold water. Change the water every hour to keep surface cold. Allow 30 minutes per pound.

• Prepare bird by first removing neck and giblets from body and neck cavity. Rinse turkey, inside and out, with cold water. Use paper towels to dry off turkey and wipe juices. Wash hands, utensils, and work area with hot, soapy water.

• Once the turkey is ready to roast, tuck the legs under the loose flap of skin (see photo 1). Or, if you're turkey is trimmed, tie the legs together with heavy string. Lift the wingtips up and over back, and tuck them under the bird (see photo 2).

• Roast turkey at or above 325°. Cook until thermometer inserted in thickest part of thigh reaches 180°. If you've stuffed the turkey, the stuffing should reach 165°. If you're cooking a turkey breast, the temperature should reach 170°. (Leave thermometer in 5 minutes for an accurate reading.) Allow the roasted turkey to "rest" out of the oven 20 minutes before carving to allow juices to be reabsorbed.

• Do not stuff the turkey the night before roasting. To prepare ahead, refrigerate moist ingredients for the stuffing and store dry ingredients in a separate container. Stuff the turkey loosely just before baking. If you pack it tightly, heat will not adequately penetrate the dense stuffing, and it will take a very long time for the stuffing to reach 165°. Never stuff a turkey that will be microwaved. The stuffing may not cook through.

• Remove stuffing from turkey before storing. Cut meat from bones within 2 hours of cooking. Refrigerate turkey and stuffing in separate shallow containers.

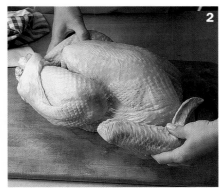

133

**ROAST TURKEY WITH THYME BUTTER AND SHALLOTS,
LAST-MINUTE GRAVY, WALNUT-CRANBERRY SAUCE,
APPLE SALAD, ROASTED AND SMASHED SWEET POTATOES,
AND RUSTIC CORN DRESSING**

GRATIN OF BROCCOLI IN BÉCHAMEL

A gratin is simply a dish, savory or sweet, that's finished under a broiler to create a golden crust. Sometimes the crust comes from breadcrumbs; sometimes it's merely cheese, as in this delicious side dish bathed in béchamel sauce.

2½ pounds fresh broccoli, cut into spears
3   tablespoons butter or margarine
3   tablespoons all-purpose flour
2   cups milk
2   tablespoons stone-ground mustard
⅛   teaspoon salt
⅛   teaspoon freshly grated or ground nutmeg
⅛   teaspoon pepper
1   cup (4 ounces) shredded Gruyère cheese

Arrange broccoli in a steamer basket over boiling water. Cover and steam 10 minutes or just until broccoli is tender. Remove from heat. Transfer broccoli to a lightly greased 2-quart gratin or other shallow baking dish.

Meanwhile, melt butter in a heavy saucepan over medium heat; add flour, stirring mixture until smooth. Cook 1 minute, stirring constantly. Gradually add milk, stirring constantly. Cook, stirring constantly, until sauce is thickened and bubbly. Remove from heat; stir in mustard and next 3 ingredients. Pour sauce over broccoli; sprinkle with cheese. Broil 5½ inches from heat 6 to 8 minutes or until lightly browned. Serve hot. Yield: 8 servings.

SHREDDED BRUSSELS SPROUTS

Caramelized onions and a tangy-sweet sauce breathe new life into these sprouts.

2   pounds brussels sprouts
2   tablespoons butter or margarine
2   tablespoons olive oil
2   garlic cloves, minced
½   small red onion, cut into slivers (½ cup)
½   teaspoon salt
½   teaspoon pepper
¼   cup plus 2 tablespoons red wine vinegar
1½   tablespoons brown sugar

Wash brussels sprouts; remove discolored leaves. Cut off stem ends, and thinly slice brussels sprouts. (They should look shredded.)

Heat butter and oil in a large deep skillet or Dutch oven over medium-high heat until hot. Add shredded brussels sprouts, garlic, and onion slivers.

Sauté 8 to 10 minutes or until brussels sprouts are tender and onion is lightly caramelized. Season with salt and pepper; transfer to a serving bowl. Add vinegar and brown sugar to skillet. Simmer over medium heat 30 seconds; pour over brussels sprouts, and toss gently. Serve hot. Yield: 8 servings.

copper accents

Copper blends well with the colors of Christmas. And this menu displays a subtle copper scheme. Various serving pieces, the place cards, the chandelier decorations, and even the desserts carry the copper shade.

place cards Let place cards be a warm welcome to your holiday table. Show off the simplicity of fresh produce: Buy small Seckel pears and rub them with the copper Rub 'n Buff paint. Then look for copper "T" garden labels or place cards at a garden shop and write names on labels using a ballpoint pen. Insert the pointed ends of labels into painted pears. You can use the same tags to introduce recipes, as we did for the pecan pie in this menu (see photo, next page).

chandelier can-do Pressed for space on the table? Then transform your chandelier into a centerpiece, allowing your family and guests freedom for easy visiting across the table during the meal. (Or, if space permits, extend your arrangements from tabletop to overhead, as we did.)

We wrapped ribbon around rims of antique copper cups and strung the cups to the chandelier. Then we added a splash of water to the cups and filled them with cut flowers, greenery, and seasonal berries. (Don't fill cups too full with water or flowers, or they may be too heavy to suspend safely from a chandelier.)

DEEP-DISH PECAN PIE

This is the grande dame of pecan pies. It slices best when chilled and served the next day. Make your servings small for this pecan-packed decadent dessert.

1	cup butter or margarine, softened
2	(3-ounce) packages cream cheese, softened
2	cups all-purpose flour
¼	cup sugar
1	(16-ounce) bottle light corn syrup (2 cups)
1½	cups firmly packed light brown sugar
⅓	cup butter or margarine, melted
4	large eggs, lightly beaten
4	egg yolks, lightly beaten
1	tablespoon vanilla extract
½	teaspoon salt
3½	cups pecan pieces or halves

Beat 1 cup butter and cream cheese at medium speed with an electric mixer until creamy. Gradually add flour and ¼ cup sugar, beating well. Shape dough into a flat disc; cover and chill 15 minutes. Roll chilled dough into a 13-inch circle; carefully transfer to an ungreased 9-inch springform pan. (We recommend covering the outside of your springform pan with aluminum foil before filling and baking this pie. It's a safeguard against leaks.) Press dough up sides of pan. Cover and chill.

Combine corn syrup, brown sugar, and melted butter in a large bowl; stir well with a wire whisk. Add eggs, egg yolks, vanilla, and salt; stir well. Stir in pecans. Pour filling into unbaked pastry-lined pan.

Bake at 375° for 15 minutes. Reduce oven temperature to 300°; bake 2 hours and 15 minutes, shielding pie with aluminum foil to prevent excess browning, if necessary. Cool completely on a wire rack. Cover and chill, if desired. Remove sides of springform pan to serve. Yield: 1 (9-inch) pie.

CHEESECAKE FLAN

Savoring the contrast between this incredibly rich baked custard and its slightly burnt-tasting caramel sauce is a delicious experience.

¾	cup sugar
4	large eggs
3	slices white bread, crusts removed
1	(14-ounce) can sweetened condensed milk
1	(8-ounce) container mascarpone cheese (1 cup)
1	cup evaporated milk
⅔	cup water
3	tablespoons butter or margarine, melted
1	teaspoon vanilla extract

Sprinkle sugar in a heavy skillet. Cook over medium heat, stirring constantly with a wooden spoon, until sugar melts and turns light brown. Remove from heat. Quickly pour hot caramel into a 9-inch round cakepan, tilting to coat bottom; set pan aside. (Caramel will harden and crack.)

Combine eggs and remaining 7 ingredients in a large food processor or blender. Process just until smooth, stopping to scrape down sides. Pour custard mixture over syrup in cakepan. Place cakepan in a large shallow pan. Cover cakepan with aluminum foil. Add hot water to shallow pan to a depth of 1 inch. Bake at 350° for 50 to 55 minutes or until a knife inserted off center comes out clean. (Center should still be slightly liquid; flan will finish cooking as it cools.)

Remove cakepan from water bath; cool flan completely on a wire rack. Cover and chill several hours or overnight. Loosen edges of flan with a spatula; invert onto a rimmed serving plate, letting caramel sauce drizzle over the top. Yield: 1 (9-inch) flan.

Note: We found that a large food processor worked best for blending this flan. Otherwise we recommend using a blender.

---

ice cream ideas

If you're looking for a dollop of something to top the Deep-Dish Pecan Pie, stir up one of these fancy flavored ice creams. Freeze the cream several hours, or days, before your big holiday meal.

FLAVORED CREAM

3	cups vanilla ice cream, softened
3	tablespoons Frangelico or Kahlúa, or ¼ cup spiced rum, or 1½ tablespoons instant espresso coffee granules

Place ice cream in a large bowl. Drizzle with desired liqueur, or sprinkle with coffee granules; stir well. Spoon ice cream into individual storage containers, cover, and freeze until firm. To serve, spoon small dollops of ice cream onto pie. Yield: 3 cups.

Note: Ice cream stores easily in small amounts in disposable, rigid plastic containers available at large supermarkets.

DEEP-DISH PECAN PIE (ABOVE) AND
CHEESECAKE FLAN

terrific tablescapes

USE WHAT YOU HAVE, BORROW FROM
FRIENDS, OR SPLURGE ON SOMETHING
NEW—WHICHEVER WAY YOU CHOOSE, GATHER
INSPIRATION FROM THESE PAGES TO SET A
STUNNING HOLIDAY TABLE.

a fragrant blend for the table

This tablescape fills the air with the aroma of paperwhites and fresh evergreens. The arrangement should last up to a week; however, you may need to replace the cut greenery and the water in the flower vases.

To create the design, place potted paperwhites along the center of the table. Tie ribbons around the pots for added color. Around the pots, accent with a variety of silver and red ornaments, votive candles, greenery, and fresh tulips in small vases. Loop red star wire through the grouping for more color. Mirrored squares and glass blocks reflect the candlelight and enhance the sparkle.

To pot your own paperwhites with rye grass as shown here, about a month before you want them to bloom, fill a pot about three-fourths full with potting soil. Fill the top of the pot with paperwhite bulbs. Pour gravel around the bulbs to hold them in place, leaving the tips of the bulbs uncovered. Cover with soil. Water well, and repeat when the soil feels dry. Place pots in a sunny location. Wait two weeks; then sprinkle ryegrass seeds on the topsoil of the pot. Water gently. Grass should germinate in about two weeks along with bulbs. If you prefer, purchase paperwhites already in bloom at nurseries, florists, and the floral department of larger grocery stores.

QUICK CANDLES

To make a cranberry candle like the one pictured in the center of the arrangement, fill a glass cylinder about one-third full with fresh cranberries. Add water to desired level in vase. Place a floating candle in the cylinder.

a berry delightful tablescape

Assemble a festive forest with berry and twig trees, votive candles, and fresh greenery. Purchase berry trees, or make your own by tucking berry sprigs into a grapevine tree form (both types of trees can be found at crafts and discount stores). At the windows are a bountiful swag and two wreaths of seeded eucalyptus, all hung with holiday ribbon. Seeded eucalyptus is available from florist shops, but evergreen clippings from the yard can be equally charming.

deck your chairs

Wreath For a classic decoration, cover a small plastic foam or florist foam wreath form with magnolia leaves and cedar. Add roses as accents, and attach the wreath to the chair with a bow.

Stocking A simple stocking takes a starring role as a chair adornment. Tie the stocking to the chair, and tuck a wrapped party favor inside.

Buckets Greenery and berries bring Christmas cheer to the table. Place moistened florist foam inside a heavy-duty plastic bag, and put the foam and bag in a narrow bucket. Stick stems in the foam to keep greenery fresh for several days.

★ CHAIR TIPS

• If you have time to do only one chair, make it the seat for the guest of honor.
• If you're not planning a seated dinner, dress your dining room chairs and pull them into the living room or family room. They'll make festive seating for a cocktail party or open house.
• Use these creative ideas for dressing up a chair in the guest bedroom, too. Your overnight company will feel like royalty.
• Be sure that any wires used to attach chair decorations are well secured so that your guests—or their new holiday sweaters—won't accidentally get hooked.

glamour in a fishbowl

There's an understated elegance to white flowers. Here, tulips and orchids pair beautifully for a deceptively easy centerpiece. Place a cylinder inside a large fishbowl, and add ornaments around it for sparkle. Fill the cylinder with water, and place the flower stems inside. Tie the look together with candlelight and ribbon. Place floating-candle holders close to the place settings to make the glow intimate. Let gilt-edged ribbons meander around the table to add casual charm. Wrap each napkin with a ribbon to complete the festive setting.

TIP Keep the arrangement cool until party time so the tulips stay budded.

floating-candle holders
easy to make and fun to give

materials
4-inch glass fishbowls • clear glass jewels with flat backs
hot-glue gun and glue sticks • floating candles

1 Glue jewels in a circular pattern around the top of a 4-inch glass fishbowl, leaving space between jewels. Working from the top down, attach the next row of jewels, staggering them between the jewels of the upper row. Continue the process until the bowl is covered from top to bottom.

2 Fill the bowl half full with water, and place a small floating candle inside. Send a floating-candle holder home with each guest as a holiday party favor.

143

a package deal

Tie up a quick centerpiece that's also easy on the budget. Wrap empty boxes (or use real presents if you like), and stack them along the center of the dining table. For combination place card/party favors, wrap small boxes (without their tops), and fill with treats. Put a place card in each box. Continue the gift theme on the sideboard with more wrapped boxes and greenery.

For added holiday ambience in the dining room, hang fluffy evergreen wreaths in the windows and on the walls in place of paintings. And don't forget the chandelier! Above, abundant evergreen clippings are accented with ornaments and trimmed with cheerful red bows. Use florist wire to hold the greenery, ornaments, and ribbons in place.

5 steps to a quick tablescape

1. Cut several pieces of greenery from the yard with sharp pruners, or visit local florist and garden shops for a variety of greenery. Allow cut stems to soak in tepid water overnight. Depending on your arrangement, you may be able to conceal cut ends in water-filled florist picks.

2. Create a focal point on a tabletop or countertop using tall candles, topiaries, or a medium-size gift basket.

3. Surround the focal point with cut greenery and other fresh items, such as fruit, nuts, or pinecones.

4. Add decorations—such as berries, tea lights, holiday ornaments, bells, candy canes, or ribbons—around the edges of your tablescape.

5. Remove greenery pieces as they fade, and replace them with fresh clippings.

beyond red and green

Upstage the traditional color scheme of Christmas with garlands and ornaments in vivid jewel tones. The stylish approach shown here is easy—it's all in the details, each reinforcing the unique tones of the overall arrangement.

Place a generous swath of regal purple fabric down the center of the table, folding under the raw edges. Trail a beaded garland along the center of the fabric. Fill in with cranberry, pistachio green, and amber glassware to hold ornaments and flowers. Light votive candles inside vibrant red holders to make the whole centerpiece twinkle.

ORNAMENT PLACE CARDS

Trim colored paper with decorative-edge scissors, and wire the personalized tags to ornaments. Tie the ornaments to the chandelier with ribbon.

no-sew tablecloths
quick ideas for the holidays

Set your table with a beautiful cloth, and you're off to a great start. These table coverings are quick to make and the finished products are versatile enough to be used on rectangular, round, or square tables.

square table topper

materials
hot-glue gun and glue sticks • 1½ yards of 54-inch-wide fabric • 6 yards of bullion fringe • 6 yards of decorative cording

1 Use hot glue and a hot-glue gun to apply dots of glue to the edge of the fabric, starting at the center of one side. Press the heading of the bullion fringe onto the dots of glue for several seconds to secure. At the corners of the fabric, fold the heading down at a 45-degree angle so that it will lie flat. Continue around the edges of the fabric until all sides are covered. (If the glue comes through the fabric, press the heading down using a folded washcloth.)

2 Apply dots of hot glue to the heading of the bullion fringe. Press the cording onto the glue to secure. Cover the heading with cording on all sides of the fabric. Apply an extra dot of glue where the cording ends intersect.

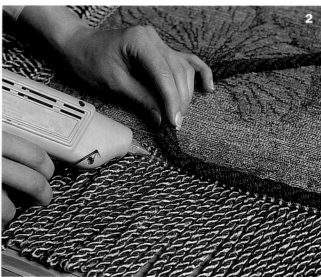

corded table runner

materials

hot-glue gun and glue sticks • 2¼ yards of fabric • 5 yards of cording

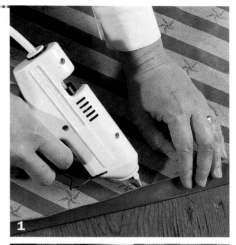

1 For an 82-inch table runner, cut the width of the runner approximately 18 inches to 20 inches, using your table and the fabric's design as a guide to an appealing width. Allow 1 inch extra on each side to fold under. Taper the ends on a 45-degree angle. Fold under 1 inch on all sides, and press. Hot-glue the hem.

2 Apply dots of hot glue to the hem. Press the decorative cording to the outside edges of the runner to secure.

3 Check as you glue the decorative cording to make sure the cording is even and visible on the right side of the table runner.

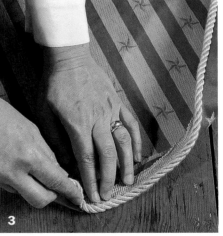

PAINT YOUR GLASSES

Use gold paint markers to add holiday motifs to clear glasses and plates. Handwash the glasses, if you want to keep the design; otherwise, you can easily scratch off the paint with your fingernail after the party.

candle power
sparkling seasonal decorations

Cast a welcoming glow with candles in unique holders that will create a warm and festive mood. Use the citrus votives (below) for a special party. The moss and ribbon candleholders (opposite), which are made from permanent materials, will last for years.

citrus votive

materials
navel oranges • kitchen knife • spoon • ballpoint pen • craft knife • tea lights

1 Make citrus votives the day before your party. Slice off the top (navel end) of the orange. Use a sharp kitchen knife to cut around the inside perimeter of the orange. Gently scoop out the pulp with a spoon. Remove all the citrus flesh, leaving only the white pith inside the orange shell.

2 With a ballpoint pen, draw a small star on the orange skin. Use a sharp craft knife to cut out the pattern. Fill the hollowed shells with damp paper towels. Encase each orange in plastic wrap, and store in the refrigerator overnight. Unwrap, and place a tea light inside the orange when ready to use.

moss and ribbon candleholders

To enable the moss candleholder to fit securely onto a conventional candlestick, push a 2- to 3-inch nail through the small end of a cork that fits into the desired candlestick. Insert the nail with the cork into the bottom of a craft foam ball. Push a plastic candleholder (found at floral and crafts stores) into the top of the ball (opposite the cork).

Cover the craft foam ball with sheet moss, using either glue or florist pins. Glue or pin ribbons and permanent fruit and foliage to the ball for embellishment.

over-the-top decorations

PRETTY CHANDELIERS BEG TO BE INCLUDED IN THE HOLIDAY DECORATING
PLAN. USE THESE IDEAS TO CREATE YOUR OWN DESIGNS. THE SKY'S THE LIMIT!

market fresh

Shiny apples in the season's signature color add a sweet accent to the dining room's holiday look. To prepare the apples, fold an 18-inch-length of florist wire in half and push it through each apple from bottom to top. Place sprigs of seeded eucalyptus, pine, and a length of ribbon at the top of the apple, twisting the wire to secure the greenery and ribbon. Tie the ribbon into a bow.

To hang the apples, cut ribbon strips twice the desired hanging length plus 6 inches. Wrap each ribbon strip over the chandelier arm, and tie the ends in a double knot. Using the wire that holds the greenery and bow, wire each apple to the ribbon hanger at the knot. Push the excess wire into the apple. Embellish the chandelier with additional greenery and berries, as desired.

willowy charm

Exuberant use of corkscrew willow in this chandelier creates a flamboyant show. Attach willow (available at florist and crafts stores) with florist wire. (You can also use branches cut from a small tree.) Tuck magnolia leaves among the branches, wiring the leaves in place where necessary, and covering the wiring with overlapping leaves. Swag ribbon between the chandelier arms, tying bows at each light. Before your party, insert poinsettia clippings into water-filled florist picks, and set them among the magnolia leaves.

sassy centerpieces
under $20

SMART TABLE DECORATIONS DON'T HAVE TO COST A LOT TO LOOK TERRIFIC. HERE ARE SOME ENTICING EXAMPLES.

dressed in pearls

Who would think that basic corsage pins could imbue a piece of fruit with such elegance? To make the orange pomanders (left), stick corsage pins (available at crafts and discount stores) in oranges, and stack the fruit on a cake stand, or arrange in a large glass bowl. Soften the gaps with short lengths of wire-edge ribbon folded in half and twisted into loops.

simple and sweet

You'll need only a few oranges, some greenery, and ribbon for this quick arrangement (above). Stack a small cake stand on top of a larger one. Just before your party, scatter orange wedges on the plates and along the table. Place sprigs of greenery among the oranges. Swirl ribbon around the fruit and greenery. The oranges will stay fresh for about a day.

pear essentials

A single row of pears in a flat, rectangular dish (above) forms an amazingly stylish table decoration. Silky brown cording tied around the stems and a soft touch of greenery are the only adornments needed.

naturally festive

Christmas comes in living color with nature offering a fabulous assortment of red and green (opposite). The colors play easily together in a festive bowl that is filled with a potted kalanchoe, green apples, and avocados.

all is calm

Two holiday staples—paperwhites and candles—create a quiet mood in this simple setting. Three candles are nestled in sand. Two paperwhite clusters, cut just below the blooms, and a single holly berry are placed to the side of the candles. To keep flowers fresh, put them in water picks, or cover a tiny piece of moist florist foam in Spanish moss and snuggle it into the sand. Push the flower stems into the foam.

sheer savvy

• Luminous, see-through fabrics spark bright ideas for stylish tabletops. To add subtle color to your dining table, layer a piece of airy pastel fabric over a deeper hued one.

• Create a no-sew tablecloth by cutting lengths of three different-colored light-weight fabrics. Instead of hemming, use pinking shears to cut the fabrics' edges, and layer the three lengths on the table. Make napkins by finishing edges of fabric squares with pinking shears.

• Swirl a length of light fabric around an urn filled with greenery, nuts, or pinecones for an easy centerpiece.

• Dress a table with a lace panel from a fabric store. Fold the lace panel in half and lay it diagonally across the table, or scrunch the lace to create a more relaxed effect.

• Wrap seasonal fruit, such as pears or kumquats, individually with transparent ribbon and fabric, and cluster in the center of the table.

• Bunch shimmering fabric down the length of the dining room table. Accent with potted plants, such as the amaryllis pictured below, or use vases of flowers in holiday colors. Add texture with a berry garland trailing along the fabric.

sugared fruit
a treat for all ages

Tiers of sugared fruit are a traditional holiday decoration for the main dining table or buffet. Children can easily get in on the fun by dipping the fruit in egg whites and then rolling it in sugar.

materials

fruit • eggs • basting brush or small paintbrush • wire rack • wax paper • superfine sugar

1 Select fruits in a variety of colors, shapes, and sizes. For a tiered setting such as the one pictured (opposite), include grapes to dangle over the plates' edges.

2 Separate egg whites from their yolks in a small bowl. Lightly beat egg whites until frothy. Dip fruit in egg whites, or brush egg white onto the fruit. (Egg whites render the fruit inedible.) Place the fruit on a wire rack over a piece of wax paper.

3 Sprinkle superfine sugar over the fruit. For a heavily sugared look, roll the fruit in a bowl of sugar. Let the fruit dry on the rack for 24 hours or until dry.

★ ORNAMENTAL OPTION

Sugared fruit makes a wonderful decoration for the Christmas tree. Using ribbon and tacks, create a hanger and attach it to the top of a sugared apple, orange, or lemon. Hang the fruit ornament on a sturdy tree branch.

a sweet setting

This table decoration is perfect for a family dinner where kids can be creative with colorful candies while they wait for the party to begin. The secret to keeping this arrangement inexpensive is buying candy in large bulk bags.

peppermint stick votive

Peppermint stick candles shine a cheery light. Place a small dot of hot glue on a peppermint stick, and press it to a pillar candle until it adheres. Repeat the process until the candle is surrounded with peppermint sticks. Wrap the bundle with red ribbon, and tie in a festive bow. After the party, consider using this colorful collection as a mantel or coffee table decoration. (Never leave burning candles unattended.)

gumdrop trees

To make a gumdrop topiary, break toothpicks in half. Push the blunt end into a gumdrop and the opposite pointed end into a craft foam ball. Repeat the process, making sure each piece of candy is touching another, until the ball is completely covered.

Fit a piece of florist foam or craft foam into a decorative ceramic pot. Break off the curved end of a candy cane, leaving a straight piece. Push one end into the candy-covered ball and the other end into the pot. Arrange additional candy around the base to complete the project.

To make a gumdrop Christmas tree, cover a craft foam cone with gumdrops the same way you covered the balls. The finished gumdrop tree may be placed directly on the table or on top of a pot for additional height.

peppermint partyware
decorations with kid appeal

Gather the whole family to make fanciful tableware with candy cane shades of yellow, green, and red

materials

hot-glue gun and glue sticks • round peppermint candies and sticks in assorted colors • tiny terra-cotta pots • coffee can assorted wine glasses or dessert dishes • greenery sprigs tapers and votive candles • ribbon

peppermint pots Hot-glue peppermint candies around the rims of tiny terra-cotta pots. Drop melted wax into the bottom of each pot and insert a candle, securing it in the melted wax. Tuck sprigs of greenery around the base of each candle.

candy candles Hot-glue peppermint candies to the outside of glasses or dessert dishes. Accent glassware stems with bright ribbons. (To reuse the glasses, simply pop off the candy with your fingers.)

peppermint-stick vase Hot-glue peppermint candy sticks around a coffee can for a quick vase with lots of charm. Fill with flowers and greenery. The candy will last for several weeks.

appetizers

WHETHER YOU'RE PLANNING AN HORS D'OEUVRES
PARTY OR YOU NEED A SENSATIONAL STARTER FOR A
CHRISTMAS MEAL, THIS SELECTION OF APPETIZERS
WILL GET YOUR EVENT STARTED IN STYLE.

COLORFUL CHRISTMAS PÂTÉ

1   (8-ounce) package cream cheese, softened
1   (4-ounce) package feta cheese
1   cup loosely packed fresh basil leaves
1   cup loosely packed fresh parsley sprigs
¼   cup pine nuts, toasted
3   tablespoons olive oil
3   garlic cloves, divided
¾   cup oil-packed dried tomatoes, drained

Line a 2½-cup mold or bowl with plastic wrap, leaving a 1-inch overhang around edges. Set aside.

Beat cheeses at medium speed with an electric mixer until creamy; set aside. Combine basil and next 3 ingredients in a blender; add 2 garlic cloves. Process until smooth, stopping to scrape down sides; remove from blender, and set aside.

Combine tomatoes and remaining garlic clove in blender; process until smooth.

Spoon one-third of cream cheese mixture into prepared mold, spreading evenly; spread with basil mixture. Spoon one-third of cream cheese mixture over basil mixture, spreading evenly; spread with tomato mixture. Spread remaining cream cheese mixture over tomato mixture. Cover and chill at least 4 hours.

Unmold pâté onto a serving platter, and peel off plastic wrap. Serve with baguette slices or assorted crackers. Yield: 2 cups.

HERBED GOAT CHEESE TOASTS

1   (8-ounce) package goat cheese
1   garlic clove, minced
¼   teaspoon salt
1   teaspoon rubbed sage
1   teaspoon dried rosemary, crushed
¼   teaspoon pepper
1   French baguette, cut into ½-inch-thick slices
1   (12-ounce) jar roasted sweet red pepper strips, drained

Beat first 6 ingredients at medium speed with an electric mixer until blended.

Spread cheese mixture evenly over bread slices; top with pepper strips, and place on baking sheets.

Bake at 400° for 10 minutes or until cheese melts; serve immediately. Yield: 2 dozen.

Herbed Sun-Dried Tomato Toasts: Substitute feta cheese for goat cheese; add 2 tablespoons milk or cream to make spreading consistency. Substitute 1 (7-ounce) jar marinated sun-dried tomatoes, drained and cut into strips, for sweet red pepper strips.

Herbed Feta Cheese Toasts: Substitute feta cheese for goat cheese; add 2 table-spoons milk or cream to make spreading consistency.

Mediterranean toasts: Substitute tomato-basil feta cheese for goat cheese; add 2 tablespoons milk or cream to make spreading consistency, and omit spices. Top with chopped kalamata or ripe olives.

PROSCIUTTO-WRAPPED SHRIMP

Be careful not to marinate the shrimp too long. It makes them tough.

16   unpeeled, jumbo fresh shrimp
½   cup olive oil
¼   cup vermouth
2   teaspoons dried oregano
1   teaspoon freshly ground pepper
6   garlic cloves, minced
16   (8-inch x 1-inch) slices prosciutto

Peel and devein shrimp. Combine oil and next 4 ingredients in a large heavy-duty zip-top plastic bag. Add shrimp; seal bag, and marinate in refrigerator 1 hour, turning once.

Soak 8 (6-inch) wooden skewers in water to cover at least 30 minutes.

Remove shrimp from marinade, discarding marinade. Wrap 1 piece prosciutto around each shrimp. Thread 2 shrimp onto each skewer. Place skewers on rack of a lightly greased broiler pan. Broil 5½ inches from heat 7 to 9 minutes or until shrimp turn pink, turning once. Yield: 8 servings.

BLT DIPPERS

The bacon filling also makes a chunky dressing for a salad.

1   cup mayonnaise
1   (8-ounce) container sour cream
1   pound bacon, cooked and crumbled
2   large tomatoes, chopped
Belgian endive leaves

Combine mayonnaise and sour cream in a medium bowl, stirring well with a wire whisk; stir in bacon and tomato. Spoon 1 tablespoon onto individual Belgian endive leaves, or serve with Melba toast rounds. Yield: 4 cups.

PROSCIUTTO-WRAPPED SHRIMP

SPINACH-SAUSAGE TURNOVERS

Starting with convenience products like frozen spinach soufflé and puff pastry makes foolproof, impressive appetizers.

½   pound hot Italian sausage
4   green onions, minced
1   (12-ounce) package frozen spinach soufflé, thawed
⅓   cup shredded Parmesan cheese
½   teaspoon freshly ground pepper
1   (17¼-ounce) package frozen puff pastry sheets, thawed

Remove casings from sausage. Cook sausage and green onions in a skillet over medium-high heat, stirring until sausage crumbles and is no longer pink; drain. Stir in spinach soufflé, cheese, and pepper.

Roll each pastry sheet into a 15- x 12-inch rectangle on a lightly floured surface. Cut into 3-inch squares.

Spoon about 1 tablespoon spinach mixture onto center of each square. Moisten edges of pastry with water, and fold in half to form a triangle. Press edges with a fork to seal, and place on lightly greased baking sheets.

Bake at 400° for 12 to 15 minutes or until browned. Serve immediately. Yield: 40 appetizers.

Note: For testing purposes only, we used Stouffer's Spinach Soufflé. Thaw spinach soufflé in the microwave at MEDIUM (50% power) 6 to 7 minutes.

To make ahead: Assemble turnovers, and freeze, unbaked, up to 3 months. Thaw at room temperature for 30 minutes, and bake at 400° for 21 minutes or until golden. Or, bake turnovers as directed, and freeze up to 3 months. Thaw at room temperature for 30 minutes. Place on a baking sheet, and cover loosely with aluminum foil. Bake at 350° for 25 minutes or until thoroughly heated.

quick ideas

• If you're preparing all the food for a party yourself, select make-ahead recipes to avoid last-minute cooking.

• If you're running out of time, fill in your menu with food purchased from the deli such as smoked salmon, sliced roast beef, and boiled peel-and-eat shrimp. Your guests will never know you didn't cook everything yourself if you transfer these items to your own serving pieces.

• Select the trays and containers you'll need for your party; then label and arrange their positions on the table. Labels help you remember your plan if you're in a rush, but, most important, they allow others to help you carry out your plan without any supervision.

• Set trays of food that most often need replenishing close to the kitchen.

CHICKEN-AND-ARTICHOKE TARTS

Your guests will love the creamy texture and flaky crusts of these flavorful morsels.

⅔ cup coarsely chopped pecans
1   (15-ounce) package refrigerated
    piecrusts
2   cups diced cooked chicken
1   (14-ounce) can artichoke hearts,
    drained and chopped
3   tablespoons mayonnaise
3   tablespoons sour cream
¼   cup minced green onions
1   garlic clove, minced
½   teaspoon salt
½   teaspoon ground black pepper
¼   teaspoon ground red pepper

Bake pecans in a shallow pan at 350° for 5 to 10 minutes or until toasted. Set aside.

Unfold 1 piecrust, and press out fold lines; cut crust with a 2½-inch round cookie cutter. Press rounds into mini muffin pans, trimming edges as needed, and place on baking sheets. Repeat procedure with remaining piecrust, rerolling and cutting dough scraps. Cover and freeze for 15 minutes.

Bake tart shells on baking sheets at 425° for 7 to 8 minutes or until shells are golden brown. Cool in pans on wire racks for 10 minutes. Remove tart shells from pans, and cool on wire racks.

Stir together toasted pecans, chicken, and remaining 8 ingredients; spoon evenly into tart shells. Serve immediately, or chill up to 6 hours. Yield: 4½ dozen.

TIP Prepare make-ahead appetizers to have on hand when unexpected holiday events pop up. You can even share frozen appetizers with a friend as a hostess gift. Be sure to include a recipe card with baking instructions.

CHICKEN-AND-ARTICHOKE TARTS

GARLIC-PEPPER PARMESAN CRISPS

Try adding chopped fresh herbs like rosemary and pine nuts or almonds to this simple recipe for a delightful variation.

12 ounces freshly grated Parmigiano-
    Reggiano cheese
2   teaspoons minced fresh garlic
1   teaspoon freshly ground pepper

Combine all ingredients in a small bowl, stirring well. Sprinkle cheese mixture into a 1½-inch round cookie cutter on a nonstick baking sheet. Repeat procedure with cheese mixture, placing 16 circles on each sheet. Bake at 350° for 9 to 10 minutes or until golden. Cool slightly on baking sheets. Remove to wire racks to cool completely. Repeat procedure 5 times with remaining cheese mixture. Yield: 8 dozen.

BRIE WITH DRIED FRUIT AND NUTS

Semifrozen Brie is easier to handle than Brie that's room temperature.

- 1 (15-ounce) round Brie
- ⅓ cup currants
- ⅓ cup dried cherries
- ⅓ cup chopped pecans
- 1 (17¼-ounce) package frozen puff pastry sheets, thawed
- 1 large egg, lightly beaten
- Garnish: red grapes

Cut Brie in half horizontally with a serrated knife. Combine currants, cherries, and pecans. Place fruit mixture on bottom half of Brie; replace top half, and set aside.

Unfold 1 sheet of puff pastry onto a lightly floured surface. Fold corners 2 inches toward center.

Place Brie in center of pastry. Brush edges of pastry with egg; fold over Brie.

Unfold and roll out remaining pastry; brush edges with egg. Place pastry over Brie; trim excess dough. Cut decorative shapes from leftover dough; brush with egg, and arrange on Brie.

Freeze at least 30 minutes or up to 1 week, if desired. To serve, place on a lightly greased baking sheet.

Bake at 400° for 30 to 40 minutes or until golden. Garnish, if desired. Serve with thinly sliced French bread or crackers. Yield: 12 servings.

a little snack

If you don't serve the holiday meal until late afternoon, the children may need snacks to hold them over. Tempting munchies deter hunger pangs, so let the kids choose from these snacks and lend a helping hand in the kitchen.

CHEESE COOKIE SNACKS

- 1 cup (4 ounces) shredded Cheddar cheese
- ½ cup butter or margarine, softened
- 1 cup all-purpose flour
- ¼ teaspoon salt
- 1 cup crisp rice cereal

Stir together cheese and butter until blended. Stir in flour and salt; blend well. Stir in cereal. (Dough will be stiff.)

Shape dough into 1-inch balls; place on an ungreased baking sheet 2 inches apart. Flatten cookies to ¼-inch thickness with a fork, making a crisscross.

Bake at 350° for 15 to 18 minutes. Remove to a wire rack to cool. Store in an airtight container. Yield: about 2 dozen.

PIZZA SNACKS

- 1 (8-ounce) can crescent rolls
- 1 (6-ounce) package pepperoni slices
- 2 (1-ounce) mozzarella cheese sticks, cut into fourths
- 1 teaspoon Italian seasoning
- ¼ teaspoon garlic salt

Separate rolls into 8 triangles, and place on a baking sheet. Place 2 pepperoni slices on each triangle; place 1 piece of cheese at wide end of triangle. Sprinkle with Italian seasoning. Roll up, starting at wide end. Sprinkle with garlic salt.

Bake at 375° for 10 to 12 minutes or until golden. Yield: 8 snacks.

YUMMY BANANA POPS

Use your children's favorite flavor of juice to fill these fun pops.

- 4 small bananas, mashed
- 1 cup orange juice
- 2 tablespoons sugar
- 2 tablespoons water
- 1 teaspoon lemon juice
- 6 wooden craft sticks

Combine first 5 ingredients. Place 6 (4-ounce) paper cups in a muffin pan. Spoon mixture into cups. Freeze 1 hour or until slightly firm; insert a stick in the center of each. Freeze 2 hours or until firm. Peel off cups, and serve. Yield: 6 servings.

beverages

From frosty eggnog to hot cider, these holiday drinks are sure to bring smiles all around. Create a festive look by using innovative containers, glassware, ribbon, and fresh citrus. Serve your guests an outstanding beverage, and offer happy toasts for the year to come.

SOUTHERN EGGNOG

beloved eggnog

Nothing brings the glad tidings of Christmas like a cup of sweet, creamy eggnog. Settlers brought this British custom to America, where dairy farms offered a plentiful supply of milk, cream, and eggs. Inventive Southerners replaced rum and brandy with the more readily available favorite, bourbon. Thus, eggnog evolved into the beverage of spirit and spice we love so much today.

SOUTHERN EGGNOG

    2   quarts milk, divided
   12   large eggs, lightly beaten
  1½   cups sugar
    ½   teaspoon salt
    2   tablespoons vanilla extract
    ½   to 1 teaspoon ground nutmeg
    ½   to 1 cup bourbon
    2   cups whipping cream, whipped
        Garnish: ground nutmeg

Stir together 1 quart milk and next 3 ingredients in a large saucepan. Cook over low heat, stirring constantly, about 25 minutes or until mixture thickens and coats back of a spoon. (Do not boil.)

Stir in remaining milk, vanilla, and ½ to 1 teaspoon nutmeg. Pour into a large bowl; stir in bourbon. Cover and chill 4 hours. Fold in whipped cream just before serving. Garnish, if desired. Yield: 15 cups.

Note: Four teaspoons vanilla extract may be substituted for bourbon, if desired.

MOCHA FROSTY

Enhance the intensity of mocha flavor by using coffee or chocolate ice cream instead of vanilla, if you like.

    3   tablespoons sugar
    2   tablespoons cocoa
   ⅔   cup water
    1   tablespoon instant coffee granules
    2   cups milk
    1   pint vanilla ice cream, softened
        Frozen whipped topping, thawed

Bring 3 tablespoons sugar, 2 tablespoons cocoa, and ⅔ cup water to a boil in a small saucepan, stirring constantly. Stir in instant coffee until granules dissolve; chill.

Process sugar mixture, milk, and ice cream in a blender until smooth, stopping to scrape down sides.

Top each serving with a dollop of whipped topping. Serve immediately. Yield: 5 cups.

CITRUS-CHAMPAGNE PUNCH

Nonalcoholic champagne can be substituted in this recipe. See the garnish idea (right).

2 (12-ounce) cans frozen lemonade concentrate, thawed and undiluted
2 (12-ounce) cans frozen pineapple juice concentrate, thawed and undiluted
3¾ cups lemonade
10 maraschino cherries with stems
6 cups water
5 lemon slices
5 lime slices
1 (750-milliliter) bottle champagne, chilled
1 (2-liter) bottle ginger ale, chilled
1 (2-liter) bottle tonic water, chilled

Stir together first 7 ingredients; cover and chill at least 4 hours. Stir in champagne, ginger ale, and tonic water before serving. Yield: 28 cups.

HOT CIDER PUNCH

Welcome your guests with the soothing aromas of cinnamon, allspice, and cloves as this simmers on the cooktop.

1 (2½-inch) cinnamon stick
5 whole cloves
10 whole allspice
2 cups orange juice
8 cups apple juice
¾ cup lemon juice
¼ cup honey
1½ teaspoons butter

Tie first 3 ingredients together in a cheesecloth bag.
Bring spice bag, orange juice, and remaining ingredients to a boil in a Dutch oven; reduce heat, and simmer 1 hour. Discard spice bag. Yield: 8 cups.

citrus-champagne punch
preparing the garnish

materials
*citrus zester, paring knife, or vegetable peeler • lemons
limes • ice pick • wooden dowels*

1 Use a citrus zester, paring knife, or vegetable peeler to zest whole lemons in a decorative pattern.

2 Cut limes in half horizontally.

3 Poke a hole through length of the lemon with an ice pick.

4 Thread fruit onto a dowel, alternating lemons and limes.

5 Push a lemon or lime onto the end of the dowel to keep it anchored in the punch bowl.

CRANBERRY-RASPBERRY SANGRÍA

If you like a sweeter drink, add a little more sugar to your taste.

- 1 (48-ounce) bottle cranberry-raspberry juice cocktail
- 1 (750-milliliter) bottle dry, full-bodied Spanish red wine
- 2 tablespoons Grand Marnier or orange juice
- ¼ cup sugar
- 1 orange, thinly sliced
- 1 lemon, thinly sliced
- 1 cup fresh cranberries or fresh raspberries
- 2 cups club soda, chilled

Garnish: citrus rind curls

Combine first 4 ingredients in a large pitcher, stirring until sugar dissolves. Add fruit slices and cranberries; cover and chill at least 8 hours. Stir in club soda and ice cubes just before serving. Garnish, if desired. Yield: 12½ cups.

WINTER WASSAIL

- 1 large orange, sliced
- 4 (3-inch) cinnamon sticks
- 2 tablespoons whole cloves
- 2 quarts apple cider
- 2½ cups unsweetened pineapple juice
- 2 cups orange juice
- 1 cup lemon juice
- ⅓ cup honey

Cinnamon sticks (optional)

Combine first 8 ingredients in a large Dutch oven, and simmer over medium heat 10 to 12 minutes. Discard fruit and spices. Serve warm with additional cinnamon sticks, if desired. Yield: 24 cups.

CRANBERRY-RASPBERRY SANGRÍA

SPICED CRANBERRY CIDER

- 1 quart apple cider
- 1 quart cranberry juice drink
- ¼ cup firmly packed brown sugar
- 1 teaspoon whole cloves
- 2 (3-inch) cinnamon sticks
- 1 small lemon, thinly sliced

Garnishes: cinnamon sticks, lemon slices, and cranberries

Bring first 6 ingredients to a boil in a Dutch oven, stirring often; reduce heat, and simmer 15 to 20 minutes. Discard spices and lemon. Garnish, if desired. Yield: 8 cups.

breads

BAKE HOMEMADE BREAD FOR CHRISTMAS MORNING, GIFT GIVING, OR A HOLIDAY BRUNCH. THIS ALL-STAR COLLECTION FEATURES RECIPES TO SIMPLIFY YOUR LIFE BY STARTING WITH CONVENIENCE PRODUCTS, BUT THE FROM-SCRATCH OOEY-GOOEY STICKY BUNS ARE WELL WORTH THE EFFORT AND CAN BE MADE AHEAD.

CRANBERRY CHRISTMAS TREE BREAD

CRANBERRY CHRISTMAS TREE BREAD

Not only does this recipe use convenient frozen bread dough, it also uses store-bought frosting. What a time-saver!

1½   cups fresh or frozen cranberries
¾   cup sugar
1   tablespoon fresh orange juice
1½   teaspoons grated orange rind
½   (16-ounce) package frozen bread dough, thawed
2   tablespoons butter, melted
⅓   cup chopped walnuts (optional)
¼   cup cream cheese-flavored ready-to-spread frosting

Combine first 4 ingredients in a medium saucepan, stirring well. (Frozen berries do not have to thaw first.) Cook over medium-high heat, stirring constantly, until thickened (about 10 minutes). Set aside, and cool.

Roll dough into an 18- x 9-inch rectangle; brush with melted butter. Spread cranberry mixture over dough to within ½ inch of edges. Sprinkle with walnuts, if desired. Roll up dough, starting at long side, pressing gently to contain filling; pinch ends to seal. Cut roll into 16 equal slices (about 1⅛-inch thick).

On lower third of a large greased baking sheet, arrange 5 slices, cut sides up, in a row with edges touching. Form tree with additional rows of rolls, ending with 1 roll on top of tree and 1 roll on bottom for trunk.

Cover and let rise in a warm place (85°), free from drafts, 30 to 45 minutes or until doubled in bulk. Bake at 350° for 20 minutes or until lightly browned. Carefully remove from baking sheet, and cool on a wire rack.

Place frosting in a 2-cup glass measuring cup. Microwave, uncovered, at HIGH for 20 to 25 seconds or until drizzling consistency; drizzle over bread. Yield: 16 servings.

CARAMEL-NUT PULL-APART BREAD

This warm, buttery bread is best served immediately.

1 cup plus 2 tablespoons firmly packed brown sugar
1 cup chopped walnuts
¾ cup butter, melted
3 (10-ounce) cans refrigerated cinnamon-sugar biscuits (we tested with Pillsbury Hungry Jack)

Combine brown sugar and walnuts in a small bowl. Stir in butter. Spoon half of sugar mixture into bottom of a greased Bundt pan.

Cut each biscuit in half (use kitchen scissors for quick cutting). Place half of biscuit halves over sugar mixture. Spoon remaining sugar mixture over biscuits in pan; top with remaining biscuits. Bake at 350° for 30 to 35 minutes or until browned. Turn out onto a serving platter immediately, spooning any sauce left in pan over bread. Yield: 12 servings.

CARAMEL-NUT PULL-APART BREAD

MAKE-AHEAD OOEY GOOEY STICKY BUNS

1 (¼-ounce) envelope active dry yeast
1 teaspoon sugar
¼ cup warm water (100° to 110°)
1 cup evaporated skim milk, divided
¼ cup water
1 large egg
3¾ cups all-purpose flour
¾ teaspoon salt
¼ cup sugar
1 teaspoon ground nutmeg
1¼ cups firmly packed dark brown sugar, divided
⅓ cup dark corn syrup
2 tablespoons butter or margarine
1½ cups chopped pecans
1 tablespoon ground cinnamon

Stir together first 3 ingredients in a 2-cup glass measuring cup; let stand 5 minutes.

Whisk together ⅔ cup milk, ¼ cup water, and egg until blended.

Pulse flour and next 3 ingredients in a food processor 2 times or until blended. With processor running, gradually pour yeast mixture and milk mixture through food chute; process until dough forms a ball and leaves sides of processor bowl.

Turn dough out onto a lightly floured surface, and knead until smooth and elastic (about 5 minutes). Place in a large well-greased bowl, turning to grease top.

Cover and let rise in a warm place (85°), free from drafts, 45 minutes or until doubled in bulk.

Bring remaining ⅓ cup milk, 1 cup brown sugar, corn syrup, and butter to a boil in a small saucepan over medium heat, stirring constantly. Remove mixture from heat.

Sprinkle chopped pecans evenly into 2 lightly greased 9-inch round cakepans. Pour brown sugar syrup evenly over pecans.

Punch dough down; let rest 5 minutes. Roll into a 24- x 10-inch rectangle on a lightly floured surface; coat entire surface of dough with cooking spray.

Combine remaining ¼ cup brown sugar and cinnamon; sprinkle evenly over dough. Roll up, jellyroll fashion; pinch seam to seal (do not seal ends). Cut roll into 24 (1-inch) slices; arrange 12 slices in each pan. Cover and chill 8 hours or until buns have doubled in bulk.

Bake at 375° for 20 to 22 minutes or until lightly browned. Let cool on a wire rack 5 minutes; run a knife around edges of pans, and invert onto serving plates. Yield: 2 dozen.

EASY ORANGE ROLLS

½ (32-ounce) package frozen bread
    dough, thawed

¼ cup butter or margarine, softened

2 tablespoons sugar

2 tablespoons grated orange rind

2 cups powdered sugar

1 teaspoon grated orange rind

3 tablespoons fresh orange juice

Roll dough into a 14- x 9-inch rectangle on a lightly floured surface. Combine butter, sugar, and 2 tablespoons orange rind; spread over dough, leaving a ½-inch border around edges.

Roll dough up, jellyroll fashion, starting at a long side; pinch long seam to seal (do not seal ends). Cut roll into ¾-inch slices. Place slices in a greased 13- x 9-inch pan.

Cover and let rise in a warm place (85°), free from drafts, 40 minutes or until doubled in bulk. Bake at 400° for 20 to 25 minutes or until browned.

Whisk together powdered sugar, 1 teaspoon orange rind, and orange juice until smooth; drizzle over hot rolls. Yield: 1½ dozen.

APRICOT-PECAN BREAD

*This hearty, sweet bread is excellent
with a cup of tea. It freezes well, too.*

2½ cups dried apricots, chopped

1 cup chopped pecans

4 cups all-purpose flour, divided

¼ cup butter or margarine, softened

2 cups sugar

2 large eggs

1 tablespoon baking powder

½ teaspoon baking soda

½ teaspoon salt

1½ cups orange juice

Combine apricots and warm water to cover in a large bowl; let stand 30 minutes. Drain. Stir in pecans and ½ cup flour; set aside.

Beat butter at medium speed with an electric mixer 2 minutes or until fluffy; gradually add sugar, beating well. Add eggs, 1 at a time, beating after each addition.

Combine remaining 3½ cups flour, baking powder, baking soda, and salt. Add to butter mixture alternately with orange juice, beginning and ending with flour mixture. Stir in apricot mixture. Spoon bread batter into 2 greased and floured 8- x 4-inch loafpans.

Bake at 350° for 1 hour or until a wooden pick inserted in center comes out clean. Cool in pans on a wire rack 10 to 15 minutes; remove from pans, and cool completely on wire rack. Yield: 2 loaves.

APRICOT-PECAN BREAD

entrées

THIS COLORFUL VARIETY OF TOP-RATED MAIN DISHES CAN TAKE YOU BEYOND BASIC TURKEY FARE THIS SEASON. ANY ONE OF THESE RECIPES CAN SERVE AS AN IMPRESSIVE MAIN DISH TO A FABULOUS HOLIDAY MEAL.

STUFFED PORK LOIN WITH CHERRY-PECAN SAUCE

Spicy-sweet aromas will fill the air as this succulent stuffed pork roast bakes in the oven. Finish it off with a homemade cherry-pecan sauce and garnish with sage leaves. You can never go wrong with such a simple, elegant entrée.

- 1 (21-ounce) can cherry fruit filling, divided
- 2 cups herb-seasoned stuffing mix
- ¼ cup butter or margarine, melted
- ½ teaspoon salt
- ½ teaspoon pepper
- 1 (3- to 4-pound) boneless pork loin roast
- 2 tablespoons red wine vinegar
- ½ teaspoon ground allspice
- ½ cup chopped pecans, toasted
  Garnish: fresh sage leaves

Combine half of fruit filling with stuffing mix and next 3 ingredients.

Slice roast lengthwise, cutting to, but not through, 1 side. Open at cut, forming 1 large piece of roast.

Use meat mallet to pound roast to ½-inch thickness, making a large rectangle. Spoon stuffing mixture evenly over pork. Beginning at a long side, roll up pork, jellyroll fashion, and tie securely with heavy string at 2-inch intervals.

Bake on a greased rack in a roasting pan at 325° for 1 hour and 30 minutes or until a meat thermometer inserted into thickest portion of roast registers 160°.

Remove roast from oven; let stand 5 minutes, and remove string.

Bring remaining fruit filling, red wine vinegar, and allspice to a boil in a small saucepan over medium heat. Reduce heat, and simmer, stirring occasionally, 2 minutes. Stir in toasted pecans; serve with roast. Garnish, if desired. Yield: 8 to 10 servings.

CROWN ROAST OF PORK WITH CHESTNUT STUFFING

- 1 (16-rib) crown roast of pork (about 8 pounds)
- 1 tablespoon vegetable oil
- 1 teaspoon salt
- ¼ teaspoon pepper
- 1 pound ground pork sausage
- 1 small onion, chopped (about ⅔ cup)
- ⅓ cup chopped celery
- 1 garlic clove, minced
- 8 ounces French bread, cut into ½-inch cubes (5½ cups)
- 1 (11-ounce) jar shelled chestnuts, coarsely chopped
- 3 tablespoons chopped fresh parsley
- 1 teaspoon poultry seasoning
- ½ teaspoon dried thyme
- ⅛ teaspoon pepper
  Dash of salt
- ½ cup half-and-half
  Garnishes: lady apples, fresh thyme sprigs, flat-leaf parsley

STUFFED PORK LOIN WITH CHERRY-PECAN SAUCE

CROWN ROAST OF PORK WITH CHESTNUT STUFFING

Brush roast with oil; sprinkle on all sides with 1 teaspoon salt and ¼ teaspoon pepper. Place roast, bone ends up, in a shallow roasting pan. Insert a meat thermometer, making sure it does not touch fat or bone. Bake at 475° for 15 minutes; reduce oven temperature to 325°, and bake 1 hour and 15 minutes.

Meanwhile, brown sausage in a large nonstick skillet, stirring until it crumbles and is no longer pink. Remove from skillet, reserving 1 tablespoon drippings in skillet;

drain. Cook onion, celery, and garlic in skillet over medium-high heat, stirring constantly, until tender; remove from heat.

Combine sausage, onion mixture, bread cubes, and next 6 ingredients, mixing well. Pour half-and-half over stuffing, stirring gently until blended. Spoon 3 cups stuffing into center of roast, mounding slightly. Cover stuffing and exposed ends of ribs with aluminum foil; spoon remaining stuffing into a greased 11- x 7-inch baking dish.

Bake roast and dish of stuffing at 325° for 40 minutes or until thermometer registers 160°. Transfer roast to a large serving platter; remove foil. Let stand 10 minutes before carving. Garnish, if desired. Yield: 8 servings.

Note: Substitute 1 pound fresh roasted chestnuts for 11-ounce jar. To roast your own chestnuts, cut a slit in each chestnut shell. Place on an ungreased baking sheet. Bake at 400° for 15 minutes; cool. Discard shells.

well done

Great entrées rely on perfect cooking—they need to be safe to eat, but not overcooked. A roast or thick chop may look done, only to be nearly raw in the center.

Meat thermometers help you avoid such experiences. Inexpensive and easy to use, meat thermometers are sold at cookware stores and restaurant supply houses. A standard thermometer stays in the meat throughout the cooking time; an instant-read one should be inserted periodically and removed. Be sure to place the thermometer in the thickest part of the meat. Follow this guide for the best temperatures.

Beef: 145°—medium rare
      160°—medium
      170°—well done
Duck/Turkey: 180° (inserted in thickest part of leg or thigh)
Pork: 160°
Cooked Ham: 140°

ROAST DUCK WITH CHERRY SAUCE

TAWNY BAKED HAM

As it bakes, this succulent ham will whet eager appetites with a smoky, sweet aroma.

1   (19-pound) smoked, fully cooked whole ham
⅓ cup Dijon mustard
1   cup firmly packed brown sugar
35 whole cloves (2 teaspoons)
2   cups apple cider
2   cups pitted whole dates
2   cups dried figs, stems removed
2   cups pitted prunes
2   cups tawny port wine
Garnishes: kumquats, blood orange halves, dried figs, pineapple sage leaves

Remove and discard skin from ham. Make ⅛-inch-deep cuts in fat on ham in a diamond design. Brush mustard over top and sides of ham. Coat ham with brown sugar, pressing into mustard, if necessary.

Using an ice pick, make a hole in center of each diamond. Insert a clove into each hole. Place ham, fat side up, in a lightly greased large shallow roasting pan. Insert meat thermometer, making sure it does not touch fat or bone. Pour apple cider into pan. Bake, uncovered, at 350° for 2 hours, basting often with apple cider.

Combine dates and next 3 ingredients; pour into pan with ham. Bake 30 minutes or until meat thermometer registers 140°, basting often with mixture in pan; cover ham with aluminum foil to prevent burning.

Transfer ham to a serving platter; let stand 10 minutes before slicing. Remove fruit from pan, using a slotted spoon, and set aside.

Pour pan drippings into a large saucepan, and cook over medium-high heat until reduced by half. Stir in reserved fruit. Serve sauce with ham. Garnish, if desired. Yield: 35 servings.

Note: To save time, buy a cooked trimmed ham. All you'll need to do is score the thin layer of fat around the ham.

ROAST DUCK WITH CHERRY SAUCE

1   (5- to 6- pound) dressed duckling
1   small orange, quartered
2   sprigs fresh parsley
1   small onion, quartered
1   carrot, quartered
1   celery rib, halved
½ teaspoon salt
¼ teaspoon freshly ground pepper
Garnishes: fresh cherries, fresh flat-leaf parsley sprigs, orange slices
Cherry Sauce

Remove giblets and neck from duckling; reserve for another use. Rinse duckling thoroughly with cold water; pat dry with paper towels.

Rub 1 orange quarter over skin and inside cavity of duckling. Place remaining orange quarters, 2 parsley sprigs, and next 3 ingredients in cavity of duckling; close cavity with skewers. Tie ends of legs together with string. Lift wingtips up and over back, and tuck under duckling.

Sprinkle with salt and pepper. Place

duckling on a rack in a shallow roasting pan, breast side up. Insert a meat thermometer into meaty portion of thigh, making sure it does not touch bone.

Bake, uncovered, at 425° for 45 minutes. Reduce oven temperature to 400°; bake 35 minutes or until meat thermometer registers 180°. Turn duckling often during baking for more even browning and crisping of skin, if desired. Transfer duckling to a serving platter; let stand 10 minutes before carving. Garnish, if desired. Serve with Cherry Sauce. Yield: 4 servings.

cherry sauce:

- 1 (16½-ounce) can Bing cherries in heavy syrup, undrained
- ½ cup sugar
- 1½ tablespoons cornstarch
- ¼ teaspoon salt
- 2 tablespoons red wine vinegar
- 2 tablespoons lemon juice

Drain cherries, reserving ⅔ cup syrup; set aside. Combine sugar, cornstarch, and salt in a small saucepan; gradually stir in reserved syrup.

Cook over medium-high heat, stirring constantly, until thick and bubbly. Stir in cherries, vinegar, and lemon juice; cook until heated. Yield: 2 cups.

ROAST TURKEY WITH HERBS

- 1 (14-pound) whole turkey
- ½ cup fresh rosemary sprigs
- ½ cup fresh sage leaves
- 1 cooking apple, quartered
- 1 celery rib, halved
- 1 onion, halved
- ½ cup butter or margarine, melted
  Garnishes: fresh rosemary sprigs, fresh sage leaves, apple slices

Remove giblets and neck from turkey. Rinse with cold water, and pat dry with paper towels.

Loosen skin from turkey breast without detaching it; carefully place rosemary and sage under skin. Replace skin.

Place apple, celery, and onion into neck cavity of turkey. Place turkey, breast side up, on a rack in a shallow roasting pan; brush with melted butter. Loosely cover with heavy-duty aluminum foil.

Bake at 325° for 3 hours and 30 minutes to 4 hours and 30 minutes or until a meat thermometer inserted into turkey thigh registers 180°. Remove from pan, and let stand 15 minutes before carving. Garnish, if desired. Yield: 12 servings.

Note: For brown, crisp skin, uncover turkey the last 45 minutes of baking.

ROAST TURKEY WITH HERBS

PEPPERED BEEF
TENDERLOIN

PEPPERED BEEF
TENDERLOIN

1   (8-ounce) container sour cream
3   tablespoons Dijon mustard
2   tablespoons prepared horseradish
2   tablespoons whole green
    peppercorns*
2   tablespoons whole red peppercorns*
2   teaspoons coarse salt
1   (3½- to 4-pound) beef tenderloin,
    trimmed
1   cup chopped fresh flat-leaf parsley
¼   cup butter, softened
3   tablespoons Dijon mustard
Garnishes: baby artichokes, fresh
    rosemary sprigs

Combine first 3 ingredients. Cover
and chill.

Place peppercorns in a blender;
process until chopped. Transfer to a
bowl, and stir in salt.

Place beef on a lightly greased rack in
a shallow roasting pan. Combine parsley,
butter, and 3 tablespoons mustard; rub
mixture evenly over tenderloin. Pat
peppercorn mixture evenly over beef.
Cover and chill up to 24 hours.

When ready to serve, bake beef at
350° for 50 minutes or until a meat
thermometer inserted into thickest portion of beef registers 145° (medium rare)
to 160° (medium). Transfer beef to a

platter; cover loosely with aluminum foil.
Let stand 10 minutes before slicing.
Serve with sour cream mixture. Garnish,
if desired. Yield: 8 servings.

*Substitute the more common black
peppercorns for the less pungent green
and red peppercorns, if desired.

side dishes

THESE TASTY SIDE DISHES ALL PARTNER WELL WITH CHICKEN, PORK, OR BEEF—PERFECT FOR YOUR HOLIDAY MEALS. ALTHOUGH MOST OF THEM ARE QUICK TO PREPARE, THEY LOOK AND TASTE LIKE YOU SPENT ALL DAY ON THEM.

BROCCOLI WITH THREE-CHEESE HORSERADISH SAUCE

BROCCOLI WITH THREE-CHEESE HORSERADISH SAUCE

Spike this luxurious sauce with horseradish and a little red pepper. It's best served immediately, but it takes little time to prepare. You can get the broccoli washed and trimmed beforehand, and right before dinner is served, steam the broccoli and make the sauce. Broccoli and cheese have never been this good!

2   pounds fresh broccoli
1   tablespoon all-purpose flour
1½   cups whipping cream, divided
1   cup (4 ounces) shredded sharp Cheddar cheese
1   cup (4 ounces) shredded Monterey Jack cheese
2   tablespoons grated Asiago or Parmesan cheese
1½   tablespoons prepared horseradish
½   teaspoon salt
¼   to ½ teaspoon ground red pepper

Cut broccoli into spears. Arrange spears in a steamer basket over boiling water. Cover and steam 8 to 10 minutes or until broccoli is crisp-tender.

Combine flour and ½ cup whipping cream in a saucepan, stirring until smooth. Stir in remaining 1 cup whipping cream. Cook over medium heat, stirring constantly, until thickened and bubbly.

Add Cheddar cheese and remaining 5 ingredients; cook, stirring constantly, until cheeses melt. Spoon sauce over broccoli spears; serve immediately. Yield: 8 servings.

GREEN BEANS PARMESAN

    2 pounds fresh green beans, trimmed
    2 tablespoons butter or margarine
    8 large shallots, sliced
    ¼ teaspoon salt
    ¼ teaspoon freshly ground pepper
    ⅓ cup shredded Parmesan cheese

Cook green beans in boiling water to cover 10 to 12 minutes or until tender; drain.

Melt butter in a large saucepan over medium-high heat; add shallots, and sauté 12 to 15 minutes or until golden. Remove from heat. Stir in green beans, salt, and pepper. Toss with cheese, and serve immediately. Yield: 8 servings.

Note: To make ahead, cook beans as directed. Drain beans, and place in a zip-top plastic bag. Seal bag, and chill. To reheat, sauté shallots, and add green beans, salt, and pepper, stirring until mixture is thoroughly heated. Toss with cheese.

GARLIC-SWISS MASHED POTATOES

    1 (22-ounce) package frozen mashed
       potatoes
  2⅓ cups milk
    ½ cup sour cream
    ¼ cup butter or margarine, softened
    ½ teaspoon salt
    ⅛ teaspoon ground red pepper
    1 garlic clove, minced
    ½ cup (2 ounces) shredded Swiss
       cheese
    2 green onions, thinly sliced
    ⅓ cup chopped cooked ham
       (optional)

Prepare potatoes according to package directions, using 2⅓ cups milk.

Stir in sour cream and next 6 ingredients. Stir in chopped ham, if desired. Yield: 6 to 8 servings.

Note: Substitute ¼ cup Gruyère cheese for Swiss cheese.

SWEET POTATO CASSEROLE

This classic pairing of sweet potatoes, pecans, and brown sugar never fails.

  2¼ pounds sweet potatoes, cooked,
       peeled, and mashed
    1 large egg, lightly beaten
    ⅓ cup firmly packed brown sugar
    ⅓ cup milk
    2 tablespoons butter or margarine,
       melted
    1 teaspoon vanilla extract
    ½ teaspoon salt
    ½ cup firmly packed brown sugar
    ¼ cup all-purpose flour
    2 tablespoons butter or margarine,
       cut up
    ⅓ cup chopped pecans

Stir together first 7 ingredients in a large bowl; spoon into a lightly greased 8-inch square baking dish.

Combine ½ cup brown sugar and ¼ cup flour, and cut in 2 tablespoons butter with a pastry blender until mixture is crumbly. Stir in ⅓ cup chopped pecans, and sprinkle brown sugar mixture over sweet potato mixture.

Bake at 350° for 30 minutes. Yield: 8 servings.

Note: Substitute 1 (28-ounce) can sweet potatoes, mashed, for fresh sweet potato; omit milk.

To make ahead: Prepare casserole; cover and chill. Let casserole stand at room temperature 30 minutes before baking. Bake at 350° for 40 minutes or until thoroughly heated.

SWEET POTATO CASSEROLE

CHEDDAR-STUFFED APPLES

Serve this standout combination of sharp Cheddar and crisp apples with a cinnamon-raisin bread stuffing right in the red jackets.

¼ cup chopped onion
 1 tablespoon butter or margarine, melted
 2 cups cubed cinnamon-raisin bread, toasted
1¼ cups (5 ounces) shredded sharp Cheddar cheese, divided
 1 large egg, lightly beaten
¼ teaspoon salt
¼ teaspoon apple pie spice
 4 baking apples, cored and cut in half crosswise
 1 cup apple cider

Cook onion in butter in a large skillet over medium-high heat, stirring constantly, until tender. Stir in bread cubes, 1 cup cheese, and next 3 ingredients.

Spoon stuffing mixture evenly onto apple halves. (Cut a larger cavity in apples, if necessary, to hold stuffing mixture in place.) Place apples in a 13- x 9-inch baking dish; pour cider into dish.

Bake, covered, at 375° for 28 minutes. Uncover and sprinkle remaining ¼ cup cheese over apples; bake 2 more minutes or until cheese melts. Yield: 8 servings.

Note: We recommend using Gala apples in this recipe.

TART CRANBERRY RELISH

TART CRANBERRY RELISH

Serve with ham or over cream cheese with crackers for an appetizer.

½ cup sugar
 1 cup water
 1 (12-ounce) package fresh cranberries
 2 medium-size oranges, sectioned
 3 tablespoons fresh orange juice
 1 tablespoon grated orange rind
 2 tablespoons finely chopped celery
Garnish: orange rind strips

Bring sugar and 1 cup water to a boil in a saucepan over medium heat.

Add cranberries, and cook, stirring occasionally, for 3 minutes. Add orange sections and juice, and cook, stirring often, 10 minutes.

Remove from heat, and stir in orange rind. Cool. Stir in chopped celery. Cover relish, and chill up to 1 hour. Garnish, if desired. Yield: 3 cups.

...heesy grits
...! brunch.

1 cup uncooked quick-cooking grits
2 cups (8 ounces) shredded sharp
   Cheddar cheese
2/3 cup milk
1/3 cup butter or margarine
1 teaspoon Worcestershire sauce
1/4 teaspoon ground red pepper
4 large eggs, lightly beaten
1/4 teaspoon paprika

Bring water and salt to a boil in a large saucepan; stir in grits. Return to a boil. Cover, reduce heat, and simmer 5 minutes, stirring occasionally. Remove from heat. Add cheese and next 4 ingredients, stirring until cheese and butter melt. Add eggs; stir well.

Spoon mixture into a lightly greased 2-quart casserole, and sprinkle with paprika. Bake, uncovered, at 350° for 1 hour or until thoroughly heated and lightly browned. Let stand 5 minutes before serving. Yield: 8 servings.

freeze frame

Making dishes like Cornbread Dressing (recipe at right) ahead and freezing them can make holiday meals a little more merry. To prepare for the freezer, line the baking dish with aluminum foil or plastic wrap; fill and freeze. Lift frozen casserole from dish, and wrap tightly with foil. When ready to serve, remove foil and place frozen casserole back into serving dish. (If you used plastic wrap, don't forget to remove it.) Thaw in refrigerator overnight before baking.

CORNBREAD DRESSING

No holiday meal would be complete without this family-favorite dressing.

1 cup butter or margarine,
   divided
3 cups white cornmeal
1 cup all-purpose flour
2 tablespoons sugar
2 teaspoons baking powder
1 1/2 teaspoons salt
1 teaspoon baking soda
7 large eggs, divided
3 cups buttermilk
3 cups soft breadcrumbs
2 cups finely chopped onion
3 cups finely chopped celery
1/2 cup finely chopped fresh sage
6 (10 1/2-ounce) cans condensed
   chicken broth, undiluted
1 tablespoon pepper

Place 1/2 cup butter in a 13- x 9-inch pan; heat in oven at 425° for 4 minutes.

Combine cornmeal and next 5 ingredients; whisk in 3 eggs and buttermilk.

Pour hot butter from pan into batter, stirring until mixture is blended. Pour batter into pan.

Bake at 425° for 30 minutes or until cornbread is golden brown. Cool.

Crumble cornbread into a large bowl; stir in breadcrumbs, and set aside.

Melt remaining 1/2 cup butter in a large skillet over medium heat; add chopped onion and celery, and sauté until vegetables are tender. Stir in sage, and cook 1 more minute.

Stir vegetables, remaining 4 eggs, chicken broth, and pepper into cornbread mixture; pour into 1 lightly greased 13- x 9-inch baking dish and 1 lightly greased (8-inch) square baking dish. Cover and chill 8 hours, or freeze up to 1 month. (Thaw frozen dressing in refrigerator before baking.)

Bake at 375° for 35 to 40 minutes or until golden brown. Yield: 16 to 18 servings.

CORNBREAD, SAUSAGE, AND PECAN DRESSING

1 (16-ounce) package ground pork
   sausage
1 large onion, chopped
2 large celery ribs, chopped
Basic Cornbread, crumbled
1 1/2 cups coarsely chopped pecans
1/4 cup chopped fresh parsley
1 1/2 cups chicken broth
1/4 cup dry sherry or chicken broth
1/4 cup milk
1/2 teaspoon salt
1/4 to 1/2 teaspoon pepper
1/2 teaspoon dried thyme
1/4 teaspoon ground nutmeg

Cook sausage in a large skillet over medium heat, stirring until it crumbles and is no longer pink. Remove sausage, reserving 1 tablespoon drippings in skillet. Drain sausage on paper towels.

Sauté onion and celery in hot drippings over medium-high heat until tender. Remove vegetables with a slotted spoon.

Combine sausage, vegetables, cornbread, and remaining ingredients in a large bowl, stirring gently until moistened. Spoon into a lightly greased 13- x 9-inch baking dish.

Bake, covered, at 350° for 30 minutes or until thoroughly heated. Yield: 12 servings.

basic cornbread:

2 cups buttermilk self-rising white
   cornmeal mix
1/2 cup all-purpose flour
1/4 cup butter or margarine, melted
1 large egg, lightly beaten
2 cups buttermilk

Heat a well-greased 9-inch ovenproof skillet at 450° for 5 minutes.

Stir together all ingredients in a bowl. Pour batter into hot skillet.

Bake at 450° for 20 minutes or until golden brown. Yield: 1 (9-inch) cornbread (about 5 cups crumbled).

OYSTER DRESSING

Dressing may be made a day ahead. To serve, remove from refrigerator, and let stand 30 minutes. Bake at 400° for 45 to 50 minutes.

- 5 cups crumbled cornbread
- 4 cups bread cubes, toasted
- 1 (14½-ounce) can chicken broth
- ½ cup butter or margarine
- 2 medium onions, chopped
- 3 celery ribs, thinly sliced
- 1 green bell pepper, chopped
- ⅓ cup chopped fresh parsley
- ½ teaspoon rubbed sage
- ½ teaspoon salt
- ½ teaspoon pepper
- 2 large eggs
- 2 hard-cooked eggs, chopped
- 2 (8-ounce) containers fresh Standard oysters, drained
  Garnish: celery leaves

Combine first 3 ingredients in a large bowl, stirring until bread is moistened.

Melt butter in a large skillet; add onion, celery, and bell pepper, and sauté 6 minutes. Stir into bread mixture. Add chopped parsley and next 5 ingredients, stirring until blended.

Cook oysters in skillet over medium heat until edges begin to curl; drain. Stir oysters gently into dressing mixture. Spoon into a lightly greased 11- x 7-inch baking dish.

Bake at 400° for 45 minutes. Garnish, if desired. Yield: 8 to 10 servings.

CITRUS SALAD WITH HONEY-ORANGE VINAIGRETTE

Sliced citrus, creamy avocado, and tangy purple onion make an impression before the turkey is served.

- 4 navel oranges, peeled and sliced crosswise
- 2 pink grapefruit, peeled and sectioned
- 2 ripe avocados, peeled and sliced
- ½ cup thinly sliced purple onion
  Bibb lettuce leaves
- 3 tablespoons pine nuts or walnuts, toasted
  Honey-Orange Vinaigrette

Arrange first 4 ingredients evenly on 6 individual lettuce-lined salad plates. Sprinkle with pine nuts, and drizzle with Honey-Orange Vinaigrette. Yield: 6 servings.

honey-orange vinaigrette:

- ⅓ cup vegetable oil
- ¼ cup plus 2 tablespoons cranberry juice drink
- 2 tablespoons honey
- 1 tablespoon raspberry vinegar or red wine vinegar
- 1 teaspoon grated orange rind

Combine all ingredients in a jar; cover tightly, and shake vigorously. Yield: ¾ cup.

Note: Section grapefruit and slice oranges over a bowl to catch juices. Brush juices over avocado slices to prevent browning.

WALDORF RICE SALAD

An easy mayonnaise-sour cream dressing binds this pretty, fruit-studded salad.

- 2 oranges, peeled, sectioned, and chopped
- 1 Red Delicious apple, unpeeled and chopped
- 1 ripe pear, unpeeled and chopped
- 2 cups cooked long-grain brown and wild rice blend
- ½ cup chopped celery
- ⅓ cup dried sweetened cranberries or raisins
- ½ cup mayonnaise
- ¼ cup sour cream
  Red leaf lettuce leaves (optional)
- ½ cup chopped walnuts, toasted

Combine first 6 ingredients in a large bowl. Combine mayonnaise and sour cream; add to fruit mixture, tossing well. Cover and chill.

Spoon salad mixture onto individual lettuce-lined salad plates or into a lettuce-lined bowl, if desired. Sprinkle with walnuts just before serving. Yield: 8 servings.

Note: For long-grain brown and wild rice blend, we used Uncle Ben's Rice Trio. For dried sweetened cranberries, we used Ocean Spray Craisins.

pearls of wisdom

- Store shucked oysters on ice in the refrigerator up to three days for best quality. Never use them after the sell-by date.
- Oysters in the shell should be stored, covered with wet paper towels, in the meat compartment of the refrigerator. Discard any open oysters that do not close when you tap on the shell.

OYSTER DRESSING

CITRUS SALAD WITH HONEY-ORANGE VINAIGRETTE

WALDORF RICE SALAD

all-star cakes

CHRISTMAS ISN'T COMPLETE WITHOUT A SHOWSTOPPING CAKE TO FINISH OFF THE MEAL. SOME OF THESE RECIPES SHAVE TIME OFF YOUR PREPARATION BY STARTING WITH A CAKE MIX, AND EACH ONE COMES WITH A MAKE-AHEAD PLAN THAT GETS YOU STARTED UP TO A MONTH AHEAD.

make-ahead game plan

up to 1 month ahead•Bake and freeze cake layers.

1 day ahead•Prepare Easy Divinity; store in airtight container.

day to serve•Prepare Sugared Maraschino Cherries and Mint Sprigs. Prepare Divinity Frosting; assemble and frost cake.

PECAN DIVINITY CAKE

Enjoy this cake the day you make it; the Divinity Frosting won't hold up for longer storage.

Divinity Frosting
Sour Cream Cake Layers (see recipe using 8-inch round cakepans)
Toasted pecan halves (optional)
Easy Divinity (optional)
Sugared Maraschino Cherries and Mint Sprigs (optional)
Small candy canes (optional)

Spread about ½ cup Divinity Frosting between each cake layer, and spread remaining Divinity Frosting on top and sides of cake.

Arrange toasted pecan halves and Easy Divinity on top of cake, if desired. Arrange Sugared Maraschino Cherries and Mint Sprigs and candy canes around bottom edge of cake, if desired. Store at room temperature. Yield: 1 (4-layer) cake.

sour cream cake layers:

It's easier to spread frosting on frozen or partially frozen cake layers.

1 (18.25-ounce) package white cake mix*
2 large eggs
1 (8-ounce) container sour cream
½ cup water
⅓ cup vegetable oil

Beat all ingredients at low speed with an electric mixer 30 seconds or just until moistened; beat at medium speed 2 minutes. Pour batter evenly into 4 greased and floured 8-inch round cakepans.

Bake at 350° for 15 to 17 minutes or until a wooden pick inserted in center comes out clean. Cool in pans on wire racks 10 minutes. Remove from pans, and cool completely on wire racks. Wrap layers in plastic wrap, and freeze 2 hours or up to 1 month, if desired. Yield: 4 (8-inch) layers.

*Substitute spice, chocolate, or your favorite flavor cake mix, if desired.

Note: To prepare 9-inch round Sour Cream Cake Layers, use 4 greased and floured 9-inch round cakepans. Bake at 350° for 12 to 14 minutes or until a wooden pick inserted in center comes out clean. Cool in pans on wire racks 10 minutes. Remove from pans, and cool completely on wire racks.

divinity frosting:

1 (7.2-ounce) package home-style fluffy white frosting mix
½ cup boiling water
⅓ cup light corn syrup
2 teaspoons vanilla extract
1 (16-ounce) package powdered sugar
1½ cups chopped pecans, toasted

Place first 4 ingredients in a 4-quart mixing bowl. Beat at low speed with a heavy-duty electric mixer 1 minute or until mixture is blended. Beat mixture at high speed 3 to 5 minutes or until stiff peaks form. Gradually add powdered sugar, beating at low speed until blended. Stir in toasted pecans. Spread Divinity Frosting immediately on cake. Yield: about 4½ cups.

Note: For testing purposes only, we used Betty Crocker Home Style Fluffy White Frosting Mix.

easy divinity:

1 (7.2-ounce) package home-style fluffy white frosting mix
½ cup boiling water
⅓ cup light corn syrup
2 teaspoons vanilla extract
1 (16-ounce) package powdered sugar
1½ cups chopped pecans, toasted
Toasted pecan halves

Place first 4 ingredients in a 4-quart mixing bowl. Beat at low speed with a heavy-duty electric mixer 1 minute or

until mixture is blended. Beat mixture at high speed 3 to 5 minutes or until stiff peaks form. Gradually add powdered sugar, beating at low speed until blended. Stir in chopped pecans.

Drop mixture by rounded tablespoonfuls onto wax paper. Garnish with toasted pecan halves. Let stand 8 hours; remove to wire racks, and let stand 8 more hours or until bottom of candy is firm. Store in airtight containers. Yield: 5 dozen.

Divinity with Sugared Maraschino Cherries: Substitute Sugared Maraschino Cherries for toasted pecan halves in Easy Divinity. Drop mixture by rounded tablespoonfuls onto wax paper. Press tip of a lightly greased wooden spoon handle into center of each piece of candy, making an indentation. Let stand as directed. Place 1 Sugared Maraschino Cherry in each indentation just before serving.

sugared maraschino cherries and mint sprigs:

16 to 20 maraschino cherries with stems, rinsed and well drained
12 to 16 fresh mint sprigs, rinsed
1⅓ cups powdered sugar
⅓ cup water
1 tablespoon meringue powder
½ cup sugar

Place cherries and mint on paper towels; let stand until completely dry.

Beat powdered sugar, ⅓ cup water, and meringue powder at medium speed with an electric mixer 2 to 3 minutes or until smooth and creamy.

Brush cherries and mint sprigs with meringue mixture, using a small paintbrush; sprinkle with sugar, and place on a wire rack. Let stand 2 to 3 hours or until dry. Yield: 20 cherries and 16 mint sprigs.

THE PERFECT PAN

Sometimes you may not have the correct pan specified in a recipe. If you must substitute, use a pan with similar dimensions and volume. You may need to adjust the baking time to account for the difference in shape and size.

SHAPE	DIMENSIONS	CAPACITY	SUBSTITUTIONS
Round cakepan	8- x 1½-inch	5 cups	10- x 6-inch rectangular
	8- x 2-inch	6 cups	8½- x 4½-inch loafpan
	9- x 1½-inch	6 cups	8- x 2-inch round
Rectangular pan	11- x 7-inch	8 cups	8- x 8-inch square
	13- x 9-inch	12 to 15 cups	2 (9-inch) round or 3 (8-inch) round cakepans
Square	8- x 8-inch	8 cups	11- x 7-inch rectangular
	9- x 9-inch	10 cups	9- x 5-inch loafpan or 2 (8-inch) round cakepans
Jellyroll pan	15- x 10-inch	10 cups	Do not substitute baking sheet for jellyroll pan
Loaf	8½- x 4½-inch	6 cups	2 or 3 (6- x 3-inch) loafpans
	9- x 5-inch	8 cups	3 or 4 (6- x 3-inch) loafpans
Tube	10- x 4-inch	16 cups	10-inch ring mold or cake mold

TWINKLING STAR CAKE

The delicious combination of white chocolate, coconut, and sweetened dried cranberries makes this cake taste as good as it looks.

¾ cup butter, softened
1 (3-ounce) package cream cheese, softened
1½ cups sugar
3 large eggs
2 cups cake flour
1 teaspoon baking powder
¼ teaspoon salt
¼ cup coconut milk (not cream of coconut)
1 (6-ounce) package frozen coconut, thawed
½ teaspoon coconut extract
Nutty Cranberry Filling
White Chocolate Frosting
White sparkling sugar
Edible white glitter
Edible gold luster dust
White Chocolate Stars
Crushed rock candy (optional)

Beat butter and cream cheese at medium speed with an electric mixer until fluffy; gradually add sugar, beating well. Add eggs, 1 at a time, beating until blended after each addition.

Combine flour, baking powder, and salt; add to butter mixture alternately with coconut milk, beginning and ending with flour mixture. Beat at low speed until blended after each addition. Stir in coconut and coconut extract. Pour batter into 2 greased and floured 8- x 1¾-inch round cakepans.

Bake at 350° for 25 to 30 minutes or until a wooden pick inserted in center of cake comes out clean. Cool in pans on wire racks 10 minutes. Remove from pans, and wrap in plastic wrap. Freeze 2 hours or up to 1 month. (Freezing makes layers easier to cut.)

Cut domed top off each cake layer, using a serrated knife.

Cut each cake layer evenly into 8 wedges. Arrange 5 wedges, point side out, in a star shape on a cake plate. Place about 1½ cups Nutty Cranberry Filling inside center opening of cake wedges. Spread a thin layer of filling over top of cake wedges. Adjust wedges to maintain star shape, pressing them into filling.

Repeat procedure to form a second layer of wedges and filling.

Top each section with another cake wedge to form a third layer. (One cake wedge will remain; enjoy while completing cake.) Fill center with about 1½ cups filling. Filling should be level with cake wedges. Adjust wedges to maintain star

TWINKLING STAR CAKE

---

make-ahead game plan

up to 1 month ahead • Bake and freeze cake layers.

up to 1 week ahead • Prepare White Chocolate Stars; store in an airtight container between wax paper in a cool, dry place.

up to 2 days ahead • Prepare Nutty Cranberry Filling and White Chocolate Frosting; store in an airtight container in the refrigerator.

day to serve • Assemble cake while layers are still cold. Store in the refrigerator.

---

shape, pressing them into filling.

Spread a thin layer of White Chocolate Frosting over top and sides of cake, smoothing with a wet metal spatula. Chill 30 minutes. Set aside ½ cup frosting. Spread remaining frosting evenly over top and sides of cake, smoothing with a wet metal spatula. Sprinkle frosting evenly with white sparkling sugar and edible white glitter.

Spoon reserved ½ cup frosting into a small heavy-duty zip-top plastic bag; seal. Snip a tiny hole in 1 corner of bag, and outline top edge of cake.

Brush gold luster dust onto piped edge, using a paintbrush. Garnish with White Chocolate Stars and, if desired, rock candy. Store cake in refrigerator; let stand at room temperature 30 minutes before serving. To serve, cut each point in half vertically. Yield: 1 (3-layer) cake.

nutty cranberry filling:

1 (12-ounce) package white chocolate morsels
1 cup butter, softened
1 (14-ounce) package flaked coconut
⅔ cup coconut milk (not cream of coconut)
1 (3.5-ounce) jar macadamia nuts, chopped
2 (6-ounce) packages sweetened dried cranberries, chopped

Microwave morsels in a glass bowl at HIGH 1 minute, stirring once; cool.

Beat butter at medium speed with an electric mixer until fluffy; add melted white chocolate, beating until blended.

Stir together coconut and coconut milk; add nuts and cranberries. Stir in chocolate mixture until blended. Yield: 5 cups.

white chocolate frosting:

1½ cups whipping cream
4 cups (24 ounces) white chocolate morsels
4 (2-ounce) vanilla bark coating squares, chopped

Heat cream in a saucepan over medium heat 3 to 4 minutes. (Do not boil.) Remove from heat; stir in morsels and bark coating until melted. Cool 1½ hours. (Mixture should reach room temperature.)

Beat at medium speed with an electric mixer 4 to 5 minutes or until spreading consistency. (Do not overbeat.) Yield: 4½ cups.

Note: If frosting separates, reheat mixture, and proceed as directed.

white chocolate stars:

8 (2-ounce) vanilla bark coating squares
Clear vanilla extract
Edible gold luster dust or pearl luster dust
White sparkling sugar
Edible white glitter

Microwave bark coating in a glass bowl at HIGH 1½ minutes or until melted, stirring twice. Pour into a wax paper-lined 8-inch square pan, spreading evenly. Cool at room temperature until firm to the touch (25 to 30 minutes).

Cut into star shapes with lightly greased graduated star-shaped cutters. (Gently press each point of star, working around the star until it can be removed from the cutter.) Brush tops of stars with clear vanilla extract. Using a small, dry paintbrush, brush luster dust over stars. Sprinkle stars with sparkling sugar and glitter. Yield: 1 (5-inch), 1 (3½-inch), 5 (2-inch), and 15 (1-inch) stars.

Everyone's-a-Star Party Cake:

Double the cake layer recipe. Pour half of the batter evenly into 2 greased and floured 9- x 1¾-inch round cakepans. Pour remaining half of batter evenly into 2 greased and floured 6- x 1¾-inch round cakepans. Bake at 350° for 20 to 25 minutes or until a wooden pick inserted in center comes out clean.

Halve the Nutty Cranberry Filling

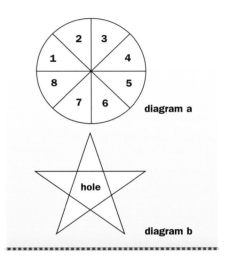
recipe; spread between 9-inch layers and 6-inch layers. Place 6-inch stack on top of 9-inch stack. Frost with White Chocolate Frosting; garnish, if desired, with sparkling sugar, glitter, and White Chocolate Stars.

Where to find ingredients: For testing purposes only, we used Nestlé Premiere White Morsels for white chocolate morsels and Craisins for sweetened dried cranberries. Sparkling sugar, edible glitter, luster dust, and clear vanilla extract can be found at gourmet grocery stores, cake decorating supply stores, and kitchen shops. Vanilla bark coating is sold near baking chocolate in the supermarket. It's often referred to as almond bark, and it comes in vanilla and chocolate flavors. Look for canned coconut milk in the ethnic foods section of the supermarket.

PECAN PIE CAKE

Leaf-shaped cutters transform refriger-
ated piecrust into flaky leaf and pecan
shell garnishes for this rich cake.

- 3 cups finely chopped pecans, toasted and divided
- ½ cup butter or margarine, softened
- ½ cup shortening
- 2 cups sugar
- 5 large eggs, separated
- 1 tablespoon vanilla extract
- 2 cups all-purpose flour
- 1 teaspoon baking soda
- 1 cup buttermilk
- ¾ cup dark corn syrup
- 1 recipe Pecan Pie Filling
- 1 recipe Pastry Garnish (optional)

Sprinkle 2 cups pecans evenly into 3 generously buttered 9-inch round cakepans; shake to coat bottoms and sides of pans.

Beat ½ cup butter and shortening at medium speed with an electric mixer until fluffy; gradually add sugar, beating mixture well. Add egg yolks, 1 at a time, beating until blended after each addition. Stir in vanilla.

Add flour and baking soda to butter mixture alternately with buttermilk,

beginning and ending with flour. Beat at low speed until blended after each addition. Stir in remaining 1 cup pecans.

Beat egg whites at medium speed until stiff peaks form; fold one-third of beaten egg white into batter. Fold in remaining beaten egg white. (Do not overmix.) Pour batter into prepared pans.

Bake at 350° for 25 minutes or until done. Cool in pans on wire racks 10 minutes. Invert layers onto wax paper-lined wire racks. Brush tops and sides of cake layers with corn syrup, and cool completely. Wrap layers in plastic wrap, and freeze up to 1 month, if desired.

Spread half of Pecan Pie Filling on 1 layer, pecan side up. Place second layer, pecan side up, on filling; spread with remaining filling. Top with remaining cake layer, pecan side up. Arrange Pastry Garnish on and around cake, if desired. Yield: 1 (3-layer) cake.

****

make-ahead game plan

up to 1 month ahead • Bake and freeze cake layers.

1 day ahead • Prepare and chill Pecan Pie Filling.

• Prepare pastry garnishes; store in airtight container at room temperature.

day to serve • Assemble and decorate cake.

****

pecan pie filling:

- ½ cup firmly packed dark brown sugar
- ¾ cup dark corn syrup
- ⅓ cup cornstarch
- 4 egg yolks
- 1½ cups half-and-half
- ⅛ teaspoon salt
- 3 tablespoons butter or margarine
- 1 teaspoon vanilla extract

Whisk together first 6 ingredients in a heavy 3-quart saucepan until smooth. Bring mixture to a boil over medium heat, whisking constantly; boil 1 minute or until thickened. Remove from heat.

Whisk in butter and vanilla. Place a sheet of wax paper directly on surface of mixture to prevent a film from forming; chill 4 hours or overnight. Yield: about 3 cups.

Note: To chill filling quickly, pour filling into a bowl. Place bowl in a larger bowl filled with ice. Whisk constantly until cool (about 15 minutes).

pastry garnish:

- 1 (15-ounce) package refrigerated piecrusts
- 1 large egg
- 1 tablespoon water
- 24 pecan halves

Unfold piecrusts, and press out fold lines. Cut 8 to 10 leaves from each piecrust with a 3-inch leaf-shaped cutter. Mark leaf veins, using tip of a knife. Reserve pastry trimmings. Whisk together egg and water, and brush on pastry leaves.

easy leaves

After cutting leaves from piecrusts, follow these simple tips to create pastry decorations for your cake.

• To ensure an even golden finish, apply a mixture of beaten egg and water to pastry cutouts, using a small artist's brush.

• Gently drape the pastry leaves over crumpled balls of aluminum foil to give them a natural-looking shape. Flatten the bases of the balls so they'll rest in place during baking.

• Wrap pecan halves with trimmings of pastry to form nutty garnishes for scattering on top and around sides of cake.

PECAN PIE CAKE

Crumple 10 to 12 small aluminum foil pieces into ½-inch balls. Coat with vegetable cooking spray, and place on a lightly greased baking sheet. Drape a pastry leaf over each ball; place remaining pastry leaves on baking sheet.

Bake at 425° for 6 to 8 minutes or until golden. Cool on a wire rack 10 minutes. Gently remove leaves from foil.

Pinch 12 pea-size pieces from pastry trimmings. Place between pecan halves, forming sandwiches. Cut remaining pastry into 2-inch pieces; wrap around pecan sandwiches, leaving jagged edges to resemble half-shelled pecans. Brush with egg mixture. Place on baking sheet.

Bake at 350° for 10 minutes or until golden. Cool on wire rack. Yield: 16 to 20 pastry leaves; 12 pecan pastries.

HOLIDAY LANE CAKE

1 (18.25-ounce) package white cake
  mix
3 large eggs
1¼ cups buttermilk
¼ cup vegetable oil
Nutty Fruit Filling
1 (7.2-ounce) package fluffy white
  frosting mix
½ cup boiling water
Holly Leaves
Assorted red candies
Candy Bow
Fruit-shaped candies (optional)
White sugar crystals

Beat first 4 ingredients at medium speed with an electric mixer 2 minutes. Pour into 3 greased and floured 8-inch round or square cakepans.

Bake at 350° for 15 to 20 minutes or until a wooden pick inserted in center comes out clean. Cool in pans on wire racks 10 minutes. Remove from pans;

make-ahead game plan

up to 1 month ahead • Bake and freeze cake layers.

1 to 3 days ahead • Prepare Holly Leaves and Candy Bow.

day to serve • Prepare Nutty Fruit Filling, and assemble cake.

cool completely on wire racks. Wrap layers in plastic wrap; freeze 2 hours or up to 1 month.

Spread Nutty Fruit Filling between layers. Set aside.

Beat frosting mix and ½ cup boiling water at low speed 30 seconds. Scrape down sides of bowl; beat at high speed 5 to 7 minutes or until stiff peaks form.

Spread frosting on top and sides of cake. Arrange Holly Leaves around top of cake to resemble a wreath. Arrange

candies for berries, and place Candy Bow on wreath. Place fruit candies between leaves, if desired. Sprinkle cake with sugar crystals. Yield: 1 (3-layer) cake.

nutty fruit filling:

½ cup butter or margarine
8 egg yolks
1 cup sugar
1 cup chopped pecans, toasted
1 cup chopped sweetened dried
  cranberries or dried cherries
1 cup flaked coconut
½ cup diced candied cherries
⅓ cup orange juice

Melt butter in a heavy saucepan over low heat. Whisk in egg yolks and sugar; cook, whisking constantly, 11 minutes or until mixture thickens. Stir in pecans and remaining ingredients. Cool. Yield: 3½ cups.

holly leaves:

1 (14-ounce) package green
  candy melts
⅓ cup light corn syrup

Microwave candy melts in a glass bowl at MEDIUM (50% power), stirring once, 1 minute or until melted. Stir in corn syrup. Place in a zip-top plastic bag; seal and let stand 8 hours.

Knead 2 to 3 minutes or until soft (about 12 times). Turn out onto a surface dusted with powdered sugar. Roll to ¹⁄₁₆-inch thickness. Cut with 1- and 2-inch

HOLIDAY LANE CAKE

HOLIDAY LANE CAKE

holly leaf-shaped cutters. Score leaves with a knife. Place on wax paper and over sides of an inverted cakepan for a curved shape. Let stand 3 to 4 hours. Store in an airtight container up to 3 days, if desired. Yield: 8 dozen.

candy bow:

1   (14-ounce) package red candy melts
⅓   cup light corn syrup

Microwave candy melts in a glass bowl at MEDIUM (50% power), stirring once,

1 minute or until melted. Stir in corn syrup. Place in a zip-top plastic bag; seal and let stand 8 hours.

Knead 2 to 3 minutes or until soft (about 12 times). Turn out onto a surface dusted with powdered sugar. Roll to ¹⁄₁₆-inch thickness.

Cut into 6 (12- x ½-inch) strips and 1 (½-inch) square, using a fluted pastry cutter. Place ends of 2 strips together to form loops. Shape each loop into a heart. Place tops of hearts together to form half of bow. Place ends of 2 strips together to

form 2 more loops, and place each on top of bow half. Wrap ½-inch square around center of bow. Place bow on side of an inverted cakepan. Place ends of remaining 2 strips under center of bow. Shape strips into streamers; place them on sides of cakepan.

Let dry at least 30 minutes. Store in an airtight container up to 3 days. Yield: 1 bow.

Note: For testing purposes only, we used M&M's and Skittles for red candies. Swiss Petite Fruit may be added to wreath.

RED VELVET PEPPERMINT CAKE

Peppermint frosting and candies update this red velvet cake that's delightfully fun and deceptively simple. Even children can take part in creating this confection.

1   (18.25-ounce) package white
    cake mix
3   egg whites
1⅓ cups buttermilk
2   tablespoons vegetable oil
1   (9-ounce) package yellow cake mix*
½   cup buttermilk
1   large egg
1½ tablespoons cocoa
½   teaspoon baking soda
2   tablespoons red liquid food
    coloring
1   teaspoon cider vinegar
Peppermint Cream Cheese Frosting
Garnishes: Holiday Trees, 6 (5-inch) red
    and white peppermint candy canes,
    crushed; 12 (5-inch) green candy
    canes, broken; 12 round
    peppermint candies

Beat first 4 ingredients according to cake mix package directions.

Beat yellow cake mix and next 6 ingredients according to package directions. Spoon red batter alternately with white batter into 3 greased and floured 9-inch round cakepans. Swirl batter gently with a knife.

Bake at 350° for 22 to 25 minutes or until a wooden pick inserted in center comes out clean. Cool in pans on wire racks 10 minutes. Remove from pans; cool on wire racks.

Spread Peppermint Cream Cheese Frosting between layers and on top and sides of cake. (Cake may be chilled up to 2 days or frozen up to 1 month.) Garnish, if desired. Serve within 2 hours. Yield: 1 (3-layer) cake.

*Substitute 1¾ cups yellow cake mix.

Note: For testing purposes only, we used Duncan Hines Moist Deluxe White Cake

Mix, Jiffy Golden Yellow Cake Mix, and McCormick Red Food Color.

If cake is frozen, thaw completely before garnishing to prevent crushed candy from running. Do not refrigerate after garnishing.

peppermint cream cheese frosting:

1   (8-ounce) package cream cheese,
    softened
1   cup butter or margarine, softened
1   (2-pound) package powdered sugar
2   teaspoons peppermint extract*

Beat cream cheese and butter at medium speed with an electric mixer until creamy. Gradually add sugar, beating at low speed until smooth. Add extract, beating until blended. Yield: about 5 cups.

*Substitute 2 teaspoons vanilla extract.

For Quick Peppermint Frosting: Stir together 3 (16-ounce) containers ready-to-spread cream cheese frosting and 2 teaspoons peppermint extract.

holiday trees:

Royal Icing
6   (4-inch) sugar ice-cream cones
12 (5-inch) red and white candy canes,
    coarsely crushed
12 (5-inch) green candy canes,
    coarsely crushed
Edible glitter or sparkling sugar
    (optional)

Spoon icing into a zip-top plastic bag; seal. Snip a ¼-inch hole in 1 corner of bag. Pipe 2 rows of points around 1 cone, beginning at large end and working

upward, to resemble a tree. Sprinkle with candy and, if desired, glitter. Repeat procedure until cone is decorated. Invert 2 cones; stack, securing with icing. Repeat decorating procedure. Invert remaining 3 cones, and stack, securing with icing; repeat decorating procedure. Insert larger candy pieces into trees, if desired. Let stand 8 hours. Store in a cool, dry place up to 1 month. Yield: 3 trees.

Note: For fuller trees, double icing recipe, and repeat piping procedure.

For the kids: Cut marshmallows from 1 (16-ounce) package in half with powdered sugar-coated scissors; cut each half into 4 pieces. Spread cones with 1 (16-ounce) container ready-to-spread cream cheese frosting. Press marshmallow pieces in rows around cones according to directions, adding frosting as necessary. Insert candy into icing between marshmallows; lightly rub additional icing on marshmallow leaves. Sprinkle with candy and glitter.

royal icing:

1   (16-ounce) package powdered sugar
3   tablespoons meringue powder
6   to 8 tablespoons warm water

Beat all ingredients at low speed with an electric mixer until blended. Beat at high speed 4 minutes or until stiff peaks form. If needed, add water, ¼ teaspoon at a time, until desired consistency. Yield: about 3 cups.

Note: Royal Icing dries rapidly. Work quickly, keeping extra icing covered tightly at all times. Meringue powder can be found at crafts stores, kitchen shops, and cake decorating supply stores.

> ## make-ahead game plan
> **up to 1 month ahead** • Prepare cake layers and frost with Peppermint Cream Cheese Frosting. Freeze in a plastic airtight cake dome.
> • Prepare Holiday Trees; store in a cool, dry place.
>
> **day to serve** • Thaw cake and add decorations.

painted dessert set

Use paint and a touch of imagination to create a colorful cake dome or other glassware for your table.

materials

glass cake stand with dome cover • grease pencil • fine-line paint writer (several)
glass/ceramic enamel paint such as DecoArt Ultra Gloss or Delta Air-Dry Perm Enamel
(We used Ultra Gloss Williamsburg Blue, Avocado, and Burgundy lightened with White.) • small natural sponge

1 Thoroughly wash and dry glassware. Begin outlining the pointed border on the outside of the cake dome with a grease pencil. Draw a horizontal line around the dome where you want the top of the points to fall. About 1 inch below, add a parallel line to mark the bottom of the points. Draw the pointed border within the lines, making 12 points touch the upper guideline and 12 touch the lower. The spacing does not have to be exact. To make corrections, erase marks with a dry cloth, and redraw.

The flower design around the dome handle is composed of 8 semicircles. Draw the first semicircle (petal), and then move to the opposite side and draw the second. To the left, draw a third semicircle between the first two. Repeat on the right side. Fill the remaining spaces with 4 more semicircles, completing the flower.

The pointed border and flower design are all you need to draw with the grease pencil. Paint remaining patterns freehand.

2 Outline the points and flower using a gold acrylic enamel paint writer. Apply all paint to the underside of the glass dome. Create the gold outline of the border and gold outline of the petal pattern. Add gold dots along the edges of the border. Draw random curls or squiggles throughout the underside of the framed area.

Paint small flower designs at the tip of each point. You can make these shapes simply by starting with a small circle for the center. Draw a series of loops around the small circle. To complete the shape, draw a second row of loops.

On the base of the cake plate, make vertical gold lines and a dotted border around the bottom. Repeat the pattern on the individual plates, being sure to paint on the underside of the glass.

3 Allow the gold to dry for 24 hours. Apply the 3 remaining colors with a small sponge. Just dab the paint-coated sponge on the inside area of the gold outlines. It's okay to stray outside the lines. And you may want to paint a second coat for more opaque color. When paint is dry, remove any grease pencil lines with a dry cloth.

Follow manufacturer's directions for using an oven to heat-set the paint. The label on the bottle may say the paint is dishwasher safe; however, you can't go wrong by hand-washing.

cookies, candies & pies

MAKE THE HOLIDAYS COMPLETE WITH AN ASSORTMENT OF SWEET TREATS TO OFFER TO YOUR FAMILY AND GUESTS. TURN CHRISTMAS BAKING INTO A FAMILY AFFAIR AND LET THE KIDS HELP DECORATE. AND WITH A TOUCH OF CREATIVE PACKAGING, FRESHLY BAKED COOKIES, CANDIES, AND PIES MAKE PERFECT HOLIDAY GIFTS.

BLACK-EYED SUSANS, PECAN PIE COOKIES, NEAPOLITAN COOKIES

PECAN PIE COOKIES

Now you don't have to choose between two of your favorite desserts. Pair the richness of pecan pie with the crunch of a cookie.

1	cup butter or margarine, softened
½	cup sugar
½	cup dark corn syrup
2	large eggs, separated
2½	cups all-purpose flour
¼	cup butter or margarine
½	cup powdered sugar
3	tablespoons dark corn syrup
¾	cup finely chopped pecans

Beat 1 cup butter and sugar at medium speed with an electric mixer until light and fluffy.

Add ½ cup corn syrup and egg yolks, beating well. Gradually stir in flour; cover and chill 1 hour.

Melt ¼ cup butter in a heavy saucepan over medium heat; stir in powdered sugar and 3 tablespoons corn syrup.

Cook, stirring often, until mixture boils. Remove from heat. Stir in pecans; chill 30 minutes.

Shape pecan mixture by ½ teaspoonfuls into ¼-inch balls; set aside.

Shape cookie dough into 1-inch balls; place 2 inches apart on lightly greased baking sheets. Beat egg whites until foamy; brush on dough balls.

Bake at 375° for 6 minutes. Remove from oven; place pecan balls in center of each cookie. Bake 8 to 10 more minutes or until lightly browned. Cool cookies 5 minutes on baking sheets; remove to wire racks to cool completely. Freeze up to 1 month, if desired. Yield: 4½ dozen.

NEAPOLITAN COOKIES

Chocolate, candied cherries, and coconut add ribbons of color to these fun cookies.

1   cup butter or margarine, softened
1   cup sugar
1   large egg
1   teaspoon vanilla extract
2½ cups all-purpose flour
1½ teaspoons baking powder
½   teaspoon salt
1   (1-ounce) unsweetened chocolate square, melted
⅓   cup finely chopped walnuts or pecans
¼   cup finely chopped candied cherries
1   or 2 drops red liquid food coloring
⅓   cup flaked coconut
½   teaspoon rum extract

Beat butter at medium speed with an electric mixer until creamy. Add sugar, beating until light and fluffy.

Add egg and vanilla, beating until blended. Gradually add flour, baking powder, and salt, beating until blended.

Divide dough into thirds; place each portion in a separate bowl.

Stir chocolate and walnuts into 1 portion; chopped cherries and food coloring into second portion; and coconut and rum extract into third portion.

Line an 8-inch square dish with plastic wrap. Press chocolate mixture into dish. Top with rum mixture and cherry mixture, pressing gently. Cover and chill 8 hours.

Cut dough evenly into 5 sections. Cut each section into ⅛-inch-thick slices. Arrange slices, 2 inches apart, on ungreased baking sheets.

Bake at 375° for 8 to 10 minutes or until lightly browned. Remove to wire racks to cool. Freeze up to 1 month, if desired. Yield: 8 dozen.

---

cookie tips

- Use shiny baking sheets; dark pans absorb more heat and can cause overbrowning.
- Most cookie dough can be stored in the refrigerator up to one week or the freezer up to three months.
- Altering the suggested pan size when making bar cookies affects consistency and baking time.
- For crisp cookies, choose the high range of the baking time. For chewy ones, pick the shorter time.
- Cool bar cookies completely before cutting.
- Cool cookies completely before storing. Store chewy cookies in an airtight container and crisp cookies in a jar or cookie tin.
- An apple wedge placed in an airtight container will soften cookies that have hardened.
- Thaw frozen cookies at room temperature 10 to 15 minutes before serving.

BLACK-EYED SUSANS

½   cup butter or margarine, softened
½   cup sugar
½   cup firmly packed brown sugar
1   cup creamy peanut butter
1   large egg
1½ tablespoons warm water
1   teaspoon vanilla extract
1½ cups all-purpose flour
½   teaspoon salt
½   teaspoon baking soda
½   cup (3 ounces) semisweet chocolate morsels

Beat butter and sugars at medium speed with an electric mixer until light and fluffy.

Add peanut butter and next 3 ingredients, beating well.

Combine flour, salt, and baking soda. Add to butter mixture, beating until blended.

Use a cookie gun fitted with a flower-shaped disc to make cookies, following manufacturer's instructions. Place cookies on lightly greased baking sheets. Place a chocolate morsel in the center of each cookie.

Bake at 350° for 8 minutes or until lightly browned. Remove to wire racks to cool. Chill 30 minutes. Freeze up to 1 month, if desired. Yield: 8 dozen.

TEXAS MILLIONAIRES

Store these in the refrigerator instead of the freezer. Chocolate can change color when kept in the freezer.

1   (14-ounce) package caramels, unwrapped
2   tablespoons butter or margarine
2   tablespoons water
3   cups pecan halves
1   cup (6 ounces) semisweet chocolate morsels
8   (2-ounce) vanilla bark coating squares

Cook first 3 ingredients in a heavy saucepan over low heat, stirring constantly, until smooth. Stir in pecan halves. Cool in pan 5 minutes.

Drop by tablespoonfuls onto lightly greased wax paper. Chill 1 hour, or freeze 20 minutes until firm.

Melt morsels and bark coating in a heavy saucepan over low heat, stirring until smooth. Dip caramel candies into chocolate mixture, allowing excess to drip; place on lightly greased wax paper. Let stand until firm. Yield: 4 dozen.

STAR COOKIE TREE

STAR COOKIE TREE

This cookie tree is impressive enough to serve as the centerpiece of your dessert table. You need access to a copy machine with an enlarging feature to make the dazzling creation. Make preparation easier by baking the cookies a day or two ahead. Prepare the icing and assemble the cookie tree the day you want to serve it.

Star templates
Star Cookie Dough
Royal Icing

Begin with a 2½-inch star-shaped cookie cutter with 8 points. Use a copy machine to enlarge the cutter by 129% to make Template G. Enlarge Template G by 129% to make Template F. Enlarge Template F by 121% to make Template E. Enlarge Template E by 121% to make Template D. Enlarge Template D by 121% to make Template C. Enlarge Template C by 121% to make Template B. Enlarge Template B by 121% to make Template A.

Trace patterns onto poster board; label each template with the corresponding letter, and cut out. You will need 2 cookies made from the cookie cutter, 2 cookies from Template G, 3 cookies from Template F, 4 cookies from Template E, 6 cookies from Template D, 6 cookies from Template C, 4 cookies from Template B, and 3 cookies from Template A.

Prepare 3 recipes Star Cookie Dough, 1 batch at a time; divide each batch into fourths. Place parchment paper on counter. Roll 1 portion of dough onto parchment paper. Dust star templates with flour; place on dough, and trim around templates with a sharp knife. Remove templates and excess dough. Slide a baking sheet under parchment paper, and place in oven.

Bake at 350° for 7 to 11 minutes or until lightly browned. Transfer on parchment paper to wire racks to cool. Repeat procedure with remaining dough until all cookies needed for tree are done. Cover and store cookies in an airtight container up to 2 days before frosting, if desired.

Prepare 2 recipes Royal Icing. Reserve 2 cups icing; add 1 cup powdered sugar to reserved icing. If desired, divide reserved icing in half, and add 1 tablespoon green paste food coloring to one of the halves. Use thin icing to frost tops of cookies; use thick icing to pipe edges. Stack cookies to resemble a tree. Yield: 1 cookie tree.

star cookie dough:

Most home-size mixers won't handle batches of dough any larger than this recipe, so you'll need to prepare this recipe three times to make the Star Cookie Tree.

1   cup butter or margarine, softened
1   cup shortening
2   cups sifted powdered sugar
2   large eggs
1   teaspoon vanilla extract
5   cups all-purpose flour
½   teaspoon salt

Beat butter and shortening at medium speed with an electric mixer until fluffy; gradually add powdered sugar, beating well. Add eggs and vanilla, beating well.

Combine flour and salt; stir into butter mixture. (Dough will be very stiff.) Cover and chill 30 minutes. Yield: ⅓ amount needed for Star Cookie Tree.

royal icing:

Prepare two separate batches of this recipe to have enough to frost the cookie tree.

3   cups sifted powdered sugar
2   tablespoons meringue powder
¾   to 1 cup warm water

Combine sugar, meringue powder, and ¾ cup water in a large mixing bowl. Beat at medium speed with an electric mixer until blended. Increase speed to high, and beat 3 minutes or until fluffy, adding additional water as needed to make mixture a good spreading consistency. Yield: 2½ cups.

FROSTED SUGAR COOKIES

Substitute refrigerated sugar cookie dough if you're short on time.

¾   cup plus 2 tablespoons firmly packed brown sugar
½   cup butter or margarine, softened
1   large egg
2   tablespoons milk
2   teaspoons vanilla extract
3   cups all-purpose flour
1½   teaspoons baking powder
1½   teaspoons salt
½   cup powdered sugar
1¼   teaspoons water

Beat brown sugar and butter at medium speed with an electric mixer until light and fluffy. Add egg, milk, and vanilla, beating well.

Combine 3 cups flour, baking powder, and salt; gradually add to butter mixture, beating well. Cover and chill at least 2 hours.

Divide dough in half. Roll 1 portion at a time to ⅛-inch thickness on a lightly floured surface. Keep remaining dough chilled. Cut dough with a 2-inch cookie cutter, and place 2 inches apart on lightly greased baking sheets.

Bake at 350° for 6 to 8 minutes or until edges are lightly browned. Remove to wire racks to cool. Repeat procedure with remaining dough.

Stir together powdered sugar and 1¼ teaspoons water. Pipe frosting around edges of half the cookies; spread frosting on tops of remaining cookies. Yield: 6 dozen.

COSTUMED SUGAR COOKIES

Let the kids help decorate these fun holiday treats. They can personalize a batch of cookies by piping their names, or they can use little candies to spell out initials.

   1   cup butter or margarine, softened
1½   cups sugar
   1   large egg
3⅓   cups all-purpose flour
   1   teaspoon cream of tartar
   ½   teaspoon salt
   1   egg yolk, lightly beaten
   ¼   teaspoon water
         Assorted colors of food paste coloring
         Decorator sugar
         Vanilla and chocolate ready-to-spread
            frosting
         Chocolate candy bar sprinkles
            (optional)
         Chopped pecans (optional)
         Melted semisweet chocolate (optional)
         Red cinnamon candies (optional)

Beat butter at medium speed with an electric mixer 2 minutes or until creamy. Gradually add 1½ cups sugar, beating well. Add egg, and beat until blended.

Combine flour, cream of tartar, and salt; add to butter mixture, beating at low speed just until blended.

Roll dough to ¼-inch thickness between 2 sheets of wax paper. Remove paper; cut dough with cookie cutters. Place 1 inch apart on ungreased baking sheets.

Combine egg yolk and water; stir well. Divide mixture among several cups. Tint with desired colors of food coloring. Keep egg yolk paint covered until ready to use. Add a few drops of water if paint thickens too much.

Using a small paintbrush or sea sponge, paint assorted designs on some cookies with egg yolk paint. Sprinkle some cookies with decorator sugar. (Some cookies will be baked plain.)

Bake at 350° for 10 to 12 minutes. Let stand 1 minute on baking sheets. Carefully remove to wire racks to cool. Frost remaining cookies with vanilla and chocolate frosting and decorate as desired. Yield: 2½ dozen.

CRANBERRY-WALNUT SWIRLS

   ½   cup butter or margarine, softened
   ¾   cup sugar
   1   large egg
   1   teaspoon vanilla extract
1½   cups all-purpose flour
   ¼   teaspoon baking powder
   ¼   teaspoon salt
   ⅓   cup finely chopped fresh
            cranberries
   ½   cup ground walnuts
   1   tablespoon grated orange rind

Beat butter and sugar at medium speed with an electric mixer until light and fluffy.

Add egg and vanilla, beating until blended. Gradually add flour, baking powder, and salt, beating until blended. Cover and chill 1 hour.

Combine cranberries, walnuts, and orange rind.

Turn dough out onto a lightly floured surface; roll into a 10-inch square. Sprinkle with cranberry mixture, leaving a ½-inch border on 2 opposite sides of dough.

Roll up dough, jellyroll fashion, beginning at a bordered side. Cover and freeze 8 hours.

Cut roll into ¼-inch-thick slices. Place slices on lightly greased baking sheets.

Bake on top oven rack at 375° for 14 to 15 minutes or until lightly browned. Freeze up to 1 month, if desired. Yield: 3 dozen.

CRANBERRY-WALNUT SWIRLS

divinity school
4 steps to a heavenly confection

Choose a sunny day to make this recipe; damp weather can cause the divinity to be chewy. Follow the tips below to take the guesswork out of preparing this traditional favorite.

1 The syrup mixture should bubble on the surface as it cools. Be sure to keep an eye on the thermometer because the temperature of the syrup rises quickly.

2 The process used when beating egg whites is as important as cooking the ingredients to the proper temperature. Start with a clean bowl. Any greasy residue in the bowl can reduce the volume of beaten egg whites. When egg whites are beaten properly, stiff peaks will form.

3 Pour the hot syrup mixture in a heavy stream, beating constantly.

4 Having a partner to shape the divinity isn't necessary, but it helps to complete the procedure quicker. Drop candy by teaspoonfuls quickly, dipping from the bottom of the bowl and using the back of a second spoon to push the mixture off the dipping spoon. (The candy starts to harden on the bottom of the bowl first.)

CLASSIC DIVINITY

There's no need to be intimidated by this holiday favorite. Just read up on our steps to divine divinity (left), and follow our foolproof recipe. Once you get the basic recipe, try our flavor variations—or make up your own!

2½ cups sugar
½ cup water
½ cup light corn syrup
2 egg whites
1 teaspoon vanilla extract
1 cup chopped pecans, toasted

Combine first 3 ingredients in a 3-quart saucepan, and cook over low heat, stirring constantly, until sugar dissolves. Cover and cook over medium heat 2 to 3 minutes to wash down sugar crystals from sides of pan. Uncover and cook over medium heat, without stirring, to hard ball stage or until a candy thermometer registers 260° (see step 1, left). Remove from heat.

Beat egg whites in a large mixing bowl at high speed with an electric mixer until stiff peaks form (see step 2, left).

Pour hot sugar mixture in a heavy stream over beaten egg whites while beating constantly at high speed (see step 3, left). Add vanilla, and continue beating just until mixture holds its shape (3 to 4 minutes). Stir in pecans.

Working quickly, drop divinity by rounded teaspoonfuls onto wax paper (see step 4, left); cool. Peel from wax paper. Yield: 3 dozen (1½ pounds).

Cherry Divinity: Substitute 1 cup finely chopped red candied cherries for pecans.

Pink Divinity: Add 4 or 5 drops of red liquid food coloring with vanilla extract.

SOUTHERN PRALINES

This is a candy you want to stay with as it cooks. When it's cooked, be ready to beat mixture with a wooden spoon just until it loses its gloss; then drop mounds quickly onto wax paper.

2 cups sugar
2 cups pecan halves
¾ cup buttermilk
2 tablespoons butter or margarine
⅛ teaspoon salt
¾ teaspoon baking soda

Combine first 5 ingredients in a large heavy saucepan. Cook over low heat, stirring gently, until sugar dissolves. Cover and cook over medium heat 2 to 3 minutes to wash down sugar crystals from sides of pan.

Uncover and cook to soft ball stage or until a candy thermometer registers 234°, stirring constantly. Remove from heat, and stir in soda. Beat with a wooden spoon just until mixture begins to thicken. Working rapidly, drop by tablespoonfuls onto greased wax paper; let stand until firm. Yield: 2 dozen.

Microwave Directions: Combine first 5 ingredients in a 4-quart microwave-safe bowl, stirring well. Microwave at HIGH 12 minutes, stirring every 4 minutes. Stir in soda. Microwave at HIGH 1 minute. Beat with a wooden spoon just until mixture begins to thicken. Working rapidly, drop by tablespoonfuls onto greased wax paper; let stand until firm.

EGGNOG TRUFFLES

The freezing steps are worth it for the delicious results you get with these truffles. They're better than drinking homemade eggnog.

8 (1-ounce) squares premium white chocolate (we tested with Baker's)
½ cup sifted powdered sugar
¼ cup butter, softened
¼ cup refrigerated eggnog
2 tablespoons dark rum
¼ teaspoon ground nutmeg
½ cup finely chopped pecans, toasted
6 ounces vanilla bark coating

Melt white chocolate in a glass bowl according to package directions. Add powdered sugar, butter, and eggnog; stir gently until mixture is smooth. Add rum and nutmeg, stirring just until blended. Cover and freeze at least 2 hours.

Let truffle mixture stand at room temperature 1 to 2 minutes to soften, if necessary. Using 2 small spoons, shape mixture into 1-inch balls. Quickly roll in pecans. Place on a wax paper-lined jellyroll pan; cover and freeze until firm.

Melt bark coating according to package directions. Remove truffles from freezer; reshape into balls, if necessary. Using 2 forks, quickly dip each truffle into melted coating. Place on wax paper to harden. Store truffles in freezer up to 1 week. Yield: 2 dozen.

MERRY CHERRY FUDGE

MERRY CHERRY FUDGE

Chocolate-covered cherries have some new competition. This easy fudge recipe contains a sweet cherry in every square.

- 36 maraschino cherries with stems
- 2 cups (12 ounces) semisweet chocolate morsels
- 6 (1-ounce) squares bittersweet chocolate, chopped
- 1 (14-ounce) can sweetened condensed milk
- 1 teaspoon maraschino cherry juice
- 1 cup chopped pecans

Lightly coat an 8-inch square pan with cooking spray. Set aside. Blot cherries dry with paper towels.

Combine chocolates in a heavy saucepan; place over very low heat, and stir constantly until melted and smooth.

---

chocolate choices

Milk Chocolate: Made of at least 10% pure chocolate, extra cocoa butter, sugar, and milk solids. Its most popular form is the candy bar; it's available in morsels, as well.

Semisweet Chocolate: Made of at least 35% pure chocolate, extra cocoa butter, and sugar. Examples include bittersweet chocolate and chocolate morsels.

Unsweetened Chocolate: Made of pure chocolate with no sugar or flavorings. Examples include baking chocolate, bitter chocolate, and plain chocolate; it's used only for baking and cooking.

Chocolate-flavored bark coating: Not made from chocolate; contains oil rather than cocoa butter.

White Chocolate: Contains no cocoa solids and is not really a chocolate. It's a blend of vegetable fat, sugar, dry milk solids, vanilla, and cocoa butter.

Remove from heat; add sweetened condensed milk and cherry juice, stirring until smooth. Stir in pecans. Spoon mixture into prepared pan. Immediately press cherries into fudge, leaving top of each cherry and stem exposed. Cover and chill fudge 2 hours or until firm.

Cut fudge into 36 squares. Store in an airtight container in refrigerator. Yield: 2 pounds.

PEANUTTY CHOCOLATE NEAPOLITANS

Chocolate, white chocolate, and peanut butter combine in one singular sensation.

- 6 (1-ounce) squares semisweet chocolate, coarsely chopped
- 1 tablespoon creamy peanut butter
- 8 (1-ounce) squares premium white chocolate, coarsely chopped (we tested with Baker's)
- 2 tablespoons creamy peanut butter
- 1 (7-ounce) milk chocolate bar, coarsely chopped (we tested with Hershey's)
- ¼ cup chopped unsalted roasted peanuts

Line an 8-inch square pan with aluminum foil so that it extends at least 2 inches over sides of pan. Lightly coat pan with cooking spray. Set pan aside.

Combine semisweet chocolate and 1 tablespoon peanut butter in a 1-quart glass bowl. Microwave at HIGH 1 minute. Stir well, and microwave at HIGH 15 seconds to 1 more minute. Stir gently until chocolate melts. Spread chocolate into prepared pan, spreading until smooth with a narrow metal spatula. (Do not clean bowl.) Chill chocolate in pan 15 minutes or just until chocolate is firm.

Combine white chocolate and peanut butter in same bowl. Microwave at HIGH

1 minute. Stir well, and microwave 30 seconds, if necessary. Stir until smooth. Spread white chocolate mixture over first layer in pan, spreading until smooth with a narrow metal spatula. (Do not clean bowl.) Chill pan 15 minutes.

Place milk chocolate in same bowl. Microwave at HIGH 1 to 1½ minutes; stir well. Spread milk chocolate over white chocolate layer. Shake pan to spread evenly. Sprinkle with peanuts. Cover and chill candy 1½ hours or until set.

Score candy into 2-inch squares. Remove from pan by lifting candy and aluminum foil by foil handles. Cut candy into 2-inch squares with a long, thin-bladed knife. Place squares on cutting board, and cut each into 4 pieces. Yield: 1¼ pounds.

PRALINE POPCORN

- 2 cups pecan halves
- ¾ cup firmly packed brown sugar
- ¾ cup maple syrup
- ½ cup butter
- 2 teaspoons vanilla extract
- 1 (3-ounce) bag butter-flavored microwave popcorn, popped (12 cups) (we tested with Orville Redenbacher's Smart Pop)

Place pecans in a large bowl. Set aside.

Combine brown sugar, maple syrup, and butter in a small heavy saucepan; bring to a boil over medium-high heat, stirring often. Reduce heat to medium, and cook 2 minutes, stirring often. Remove from heat, and stir in vanilla.

Drizzle sugar mixture over pecans, tossing to coat. Add popcorn, 2 cups at a time, stirring until well coated.

Spoon popcorn mixture onto a buttered 15- x 10-inch jellyroll pan. Bake at 250° for 1 hour, stirring mixture every 15 minutes with a large spoon. Cool completely. Store in an airtight container. Yield: 11 cups.

PEPPERMINT CANDY ICE-CREAM PIE

PEPPERMINT CANDY ICE-CREAM PIE

- 16 cream-filled chocolate wafers, finely crushed (we tested with Oreo cookies)
- ¼ cup butter or margarine, melted
- 1 pint vanilla ice cream
- 1 (8-ounce) container frozen whipped topping, partially thawed
- 12 peppermint candies, crushed
  Garnish: crushed peppermint candies

Combine chocolate crumbs and melted butter; press crumb mixture firmly into a 9-inch pieplate.

Combine ice cream, half of whipped topping, and 12 crushed candies. Spoon mixture into prepared pieplate; cover and freeze at least 4 hours. Top pie with remaining whipped topping. Garnish, if desired. Yield: 1 (9-inch) pie.

CRANBERRY STREUSEL PIE

- ½ (15-ounce) package refrigerated piecrusts
- 2 cups fresh or frozen cranberries
- ¼ cup sugar
- ¼ cup firmly packed light brown sugar
- ½ cup chopped walnuts
- ½ teaspoon ground cinnamon
- 1 large egg
- ¼ cup butter or margarine, melted
- ⅓ cup sugar
- 3 tablespoons all-purpose flour

Fit piecrust into a 9-inch pieplate according to package directions; fold edges under, and crimp.

Stir together cranberries and next 4 ingredients, and spoon into piecrust.

Whisk together egg and remaining 3 ingredients; pour over cranberry mixture.

Bake at 400° for 20 minutes. Reduce oven temperature to 350°, and bake 30 more minutes. Yield: 1 (9-inch) pie.

PUMPKIN CHESS PIE

- ½ (15-ounce) package refrigerated piecrusts
- 1 (15-ounce) can pumpkin
- ½ cup half-and-half
- 3 eggs
- 1½ teaspoons vanilla extract
- 2 cups sugar
- ½ cup plus 1 tablespoon butter or margarine
- ¾ teaspoon salt
- ½ teaspoon ground cinnamon
- ¼ teaspoon ground ginger
- ¼ teaspoon ground cloves
  Praline Sauce

Place piecrust in a 9-inch pieplate; fold edges under, and crimp. Process pumpkin and next 9 ingredients in a blender or food processor until smooth, stopping to scrape down sides.

Pour pumpkin mixture into prepared piecrust. Bake at 350° for 1 hour and 10 minutes or until a knife inserted in center comes out clean. Cool completely on a wire rack. Serve with Praline Sauce. Yield: 1 (9-inch) pie.

praline sauce:

Don't just limit this rich sauce to pie. Enjoy it over ice cream, or package some in a pretty jar as a gift.

 1   cup firmly packed brown
     sugar
 ½   cup half-and-half
 ½   cup butter or margarine
 ½   cup chopped pecans, toasted
 ½   teaspoon vanilla extract

Combine first 3 ingredients in a small saucepan over medium heat. Bring to a boil; cook, stirring constantly, 1 minute. Remove from heat, and stir in chopped pecans and vanilla. Cool slightly; serve sauce warm over slices of pie. Yield: 2 cups.

BOURBON-CHOCOLATE PECAN PIE

This decadent chocolate pecan pie is every bit as sinful if you choose to leave out the bourbon.

 ½   (15-ounce) package refrigerated
     piecrusts
 4   large eggs
 1   cup light corn syrup
 6   tablespoons butter or margarine,
     melted
 ½   cup sugar
 ¼   cup firmly packed light brown
     sugar
 3   tablespoons bourbon
 1   tablespoon all-purpose flour
 1   tablespoon vanilla extract
 1   cup coarsely chopped pecans
 1   cup (6 ounces) semisweet
     chocolate morsels

Fit piecrust into a 9-inch pieplate according to package directions; fold

edges under, and crimp.

Whisk together eggs and next 7 ingredients until mixture is smooth; stir in chopped pecans and chocolate morsels. Pour into piecrust.

Bake on lowest oven rack at 350° for 1 hour or until set. Yield: 1 (9-inch) pie.

easy as pie

• Cut extra pastry with cookie cutters for a quick and easy way to decorate the top of a pie.
• Use a pizza cutter to make pastry strips for a lattice design. Or use a lattice-style crust cutter.
• Braid pastry strips on a countertop. Carefully arrange the pastry braids around the edge of the pie.
• Brush piecrust with a lightly beaten egg before baking it to add some color and shine.

BOURBON-CHOCOLATE PECAN PIE

gifts

easy-to-make • from the kitchen • wraps

easy-to-make gifts

HEARTFELT PRESENTS ARE AT YOUR FINGERTIPS WITH
THE IDEAS ON THESE PAGES. YOU'LL FIND THEY'RE AS MUCH
FUN TO MAKE AS THEY ARE TO GIVE.

lamp toppers

Christmas-themed lamp finials are great gifts for
neighbors and co-workers. Use craft clay to form a
variety of holiday-inspired shapes. (We used
Sculpey III craft clay, available at crafts stores.) Roll
and form the clay into the desired shapes and place
on an ungreased baking sheet. Bake at 275° for
about 20 minutes. Let cool for 20 minutes. Glue
shapes to plain lamp finials with heavy-duty glue.

ornament-shaped coasters

Give these clever little gifts as cocktail coasters or as
tree ornaments. To make, cut cork into Christmas
ball shapes, and paint on festive designs with acrylic
craft paint. For an ornament hanger, bend a small
piece of florist wire, and stick both ends into the
cork. Tie a small bow around the wire, leaving room
for a hanging loop.

safety-pin napkin rings

It's safe to say that guests will be impressed with these napkin rings. Use safety pins, beads, and elastic thread to create them. Simply open safety pins, embellish them with beads, and close the pins. Run a piece of elastic thread through the top and the bottom of the pins, and tie the ends together. A set of six makes a fitting hostess gift.

button votive holders

Button-adorned candleholders bring cheer to
any tabletop. To make the candleholders, you'll
need small glass votive holders or small fishbowls from a crafts store. Encircle the votive
holders with wire that is thin enough to thread
through the holes in the buttons (found at hard-
ware and home improvement stores), then
attach shorter lengths of wire that are embellished with buttons and beads. Add twists and
loops to the wire for a whimsical decoration.
Stack the candleholders on a pedestal as a
charming display
and convenient
way to present gift
candleholders to
holiday visitors.

wineglass tags

Guests are guaranteed to keep track of wine-
glasses with these cleverly crafted labels. Purchase inexpensive metal-rim tags from a crafts
store. Use a paint pen to write names on the
tags, and then slip them onto the bases of wine-
glasses using wire. To present a set of tags as a
party favor or gift,
decorate tags with
seasonally appro-
priate words or de-
signs. Run a thin
ribbon through
the wire loops to
hold a set of tags
together.

personalized platter

Create a keepsake for a favorite family by personalizing a ceramic plate. Simple paint strokes yield lovely results, such as the pine needle look shown on this platter. Start by washing the piece to be painted with soapy water, and dry it thoroughly. Prepare the surface of the plate by wiping it with denatured alcohol. Paint the design (we used Delta Air-Dry Perm Enamel), allowing each color to dry completely before adding a second color. Use fine-line paint pens for smaller accents. Protect the finish with a clear glaze (such as Delta Air-Dry Perm Enamel Clear in a satin finish). Wash painted plates by hand. (Painted plates are for decorative

sweet party favors

Gumdrop citrus slices glued onto plastic rings make fresh-looking napkin holders—perfect for a Christmas morning brunch. Tie thin ribbon to the rings and you have party favors that hold napkins at the table and later go home with each guest to be used as ornaments.

In order to see the napkin ring/ornament clearly in our photograph, we placed it on top of the napkin. In actual use, napkins can be slipped through the circle in traditional fashion. (Our napkin rings looked pretty for over two months.)

overnight delight

Extend a warm welcome to overnight guests by placing thoughtful touches, such as fresh flowers, seasonal books, and snacks, in the guestroom. A decorated gift basket provides the ultimate in pampering. An extra blanket, warm socks, and cozy mittens or gloves are especially appropriate for cold winter days and nights (right).

plain to fancy frames

Turn an inexpensive purchased frame into a work of art by gluing on a combination of silk or dried florals, berries, cinnamon sticks, and ribbons (opposite). Experiment with different arrangements by cutting the stems apart and mixing flowers or berries from one stem with the foliage from another. Hot-glue the materials to the frame. Before giving as a gift, place a vintage postcard or holiday scene in the frame.

bath salt ornaments

Place a bowl of these relaxing treats out for overnight guests to use on leisurely holiday mornings or evenings (above). To make a set, purchase a pack of clear plastic ornaments. Remove the top from each ornament, and fill with scented bath salts, crystals, beads, or powder. Tie a ribbon through the hanging loop. Bath salt ornaments also make great gifts for teachers and co-workers.

painted pots

Paint terra-cotta pots with a variety of designs to make gift containers for plants. The pots pictured here will give you some ideas. Stripes and circles are easy to paint freehand.

To paint terra-cotta pots, use acrylic paints in your choice of colors. After the paint has dried, spray pots with clear acrylic. Fill the painted pots with your favorite winter-season blooms. Cover the top of the pot with moss to conceal the potting soil and plastic plant pots.

forcing bulbs for winter blooms

Remember someone special with ready-to-grow gifts of bulbs and all the accessories. A simple way to coax hyacinth blooms is with hyacinth vases. (If you don't have a hyacinth vase, a drinking glass or other glass cylinder that will hold the bulb above the water will work.) Fill the container with water, and set a bulb into the opening. Maintain a water level just below the bottom of the bulb.

Place containers in a cool, dark location. When the bulbs have developed roots and leaves, move them to a warm, sunny spot. They should bloom in three to six weeks.

simmering scents

Tie up a fragrant gift of simmering potpourri. In a clear cellophane bag, combine a lemon, an orange, three short cinnamon sticks, six bay leaves, and ½ cup whole cloves. Include the following directions on the gift card:

Cut lemon and orange into quarters; combine fruit, spices, and 2 quarts water in a large saucepan. Bring to a boil; reduce heat, and simmer as long as desired. (Add more water, if needed.) Any leftover mixture can be covered and refrigerated for several days to be reused.

fresh pomanders

These attractive pomanders are easy to make and are wonderful gifts.
They will stay fresh and fragrant for several days.

To make a pomander, place a rubber band around a lemon, lime, or
tangerine. Using a citrus zester, draw the zester over the surface of the
fruit, cutting next to the rubber band. Reposition the rubber band, and
continue drawing the line designs. Insert cloves into the lines you have
cut. Place cloves at regular intervals, or use them to mark points where
lines cross. Place a dozen in a tissue-lined box or wrap pomanders individually in clear cellophane tied with a bow for gift giving.

fun for all

3 great gifts your kids can make

While counting the days till Christmas, here are some easy projects that will include children in the holiday festivities.

herb tins

Purchase inexpensive metal storage boxes, and punch a few drainage holes in the bottoms (right). Cut brown kraft paper labels to fit each container, and write your message with holiday-colored paint pens. Attach the label with double-sided tape. Swap around the lids to use underneath the tins as saucers.

Choose rosemary, thyme, sage, parsley, or oregano for your tins. All are available during the holiday season.

jingle bell ornaments

Turn tiny terra-cotta pots into diminutive bell ornaments (left). Spray-paint pots red; allow them to dry. Thread a narrow ribbon through the loop of a jingle bell, knotting the ribbon at the loop. Thread the ribbon through the hole in the bottom of the terra-cotta pot. Use the ribbon to hang the ornament.

snow globes

materials

jar • figurines • oil-based paint • paintbrush • sandpaper • heavy-duty glue • water • glitter • glycerin

1 Select a clear jar—baby food and spaghetti jars are good choices. Be sure the lid fits tightly and does not leak. Clean and dry the jar thoroughly.

2 Look for plastic or ceramic figurines at cake-decorating shops and crafts stores. When choosing figurines, consider the shape and size of the jar you are using.

3 Paint the jar lid with oil-based paint. Let dry. Sand the inside of the lid until the surface is no longer smooth. Glue the figurine to the inside of the lid. Let dry.

4 Fill the jar almost to the top with water. Sprinkle in a pinch of glitter. Add a dash of glycerin to keep the glitter from falling too quickly. (Be careful when adding glycerin; if you add too much it will stick to the bottom of the jar.) Tightly screw on the lid. Turn the jar over and back again to let it snow.

gifts from the kitchen

SKIP THE MALL, AND CONSIDER GIVING GIFTS FROM THE HEART—AND THE KITCHEN. HERE YOU'LL FIND COOKIES, SAUCES, AND OTHER HOLIDAY TREATS THAT ARE EASY TO PREPARE AND SURE TO PLEASE.

VANILLA BEAN SUGAR COOKIES

VANILLA BEAN SUGAR COOKIES

These cookies are laced with a double hit of vanilla from the seeds and extract of the vanilla bean. Frost the cookies white, and sprinkle them with iridescent glitter for delicate snowflakes that make impressive holiday gifts or party favors. See the variation (at right) for how to display them on your mantel.

- 1   vanilla bean
- ¾   cup butter, softened
- ¾   cup sugar
- 1   large egg, lightly beaten
- ½   teaspoon vanilla extract
- 2¼ cups all-purpose flour
- ¼   teaspoon salt
- 2   cups (12 ounces) white chocolate morsels, divided
-     Shortening
-     Silver and white edible glitter
-     Sparkling white sugar

Cut vanilla bean in half lengthwise. Carefully scrape out seeds, using a small sharp knife. Set seeds aside.

Beat butter in a large mixing bowl at medium speed with an electric mixer until creamy. Gradually add sugar and vanilla bean seeds, beating until light and fluffy. Add egg and vanilla, mixing well.

Combine flour and salt; gradually add to butter mixture, beating until smooth. Shape dough into 4 discs. Wrap each in plastic wrap, and chill at least 1 hour.

Roll each disc to ¼-inch thickness on a lightly floured surface. Cut with 3-inch and 4-inch snowflake, star, angel, or Christmas tree cutters. Place on lightly greased baking sheets. Bake at 350° for 8 to 10 minutes or until edges of cookies are lightly browned. Cool 1 minute on baking sheets; remove to wire racks, and cool completely.

Combine ½ cup white chocolate morsels and 1 tablespoon shortening in a 1-cup glass measure. Melt morsels according to package directions.

Place cookies on a wire rack over wax paper. Pour or spread white chocolate mixture over each cookie, tilting cookie to coat completely. Sprinkle cookies with glitter and sparkling sugar. Let stand until frosting hardens. Repeat procedure with remaining white morsels, shortening, glitter, and sugar until all cookies are decorated. Yield: 3 dozen.

Giant Snowflakes: We used a 6-inch copper snowflake cookie cutter to yield 1 dozen big cookies that baked 12 minutes. Before baking, we poked a hole in the top of each cookie with a drinking straw. Once we decorated and dried them, we wrapped cookies in cellophane bags and tied them with ribbon. We taped each ribbon to the mantel, using masking tape, and then covered the tape with white plastic bags and the bags with pots of poinsettias.

creative cookie packaging

Let our cookie-packaging ideas inspire you to get started early on some holiday baking. Look for more recipes for cookies and candies on pages 196-205.

- Place homemade brownies or chocolate truffles in a sturdy tissue paper-lined box. Decorate the box with the recipient's initials or stamp the box with fun holiday designs. Close box and tie with decorative ribbon that matches the color of the tissue.
- Here's a cute packaging idea for gifts for your child's teachers at school. Stack cookies in cellophane bags; stack bags in tall glasses. Tie each bag with ribbon and add a note saying, "serve with milk" (see photo).
- Empty an oats canister. Wrap canister and lid with holiday wrapping paper and tape or glue the seams. Fill the canister with cookies, replace the lid, and tie a ribbon around the canister. Don't forget to add a gift tag with the name of the cookie recipe on it.
- Organize little stacks of sturdy cookies such as shortbread; tie them with colored raffia, jute, or heavy twine, and nestle

them in small decorative boxes. Trim each container with ribbon.

- Purchase a square bakery box from the supermarket, and fill it with an assortment of baked goodies. Add a homemade gift tag for an extraspecial touch.
- Give a sturdy white gift box with a cellophane window that hints of homemade sweets inside.
- Use your computer to design and print the recipes for your cookies to include with gift packages. Roll up the printed sheets, and tie with ribbon, twine, or raffia.
- How can you get it all done? Bake and freeze cookies up to 3 months in advance. Be sure to double-wrap the cookies securely and write the date and type of cookie on the package. When you're ready to assemble your gifts, just let the cookies come to room temperature. You can also freeze cookie dough up to 3 months ahead. Let it thaw in the refrigerator before baking.

SWEET MICE, CHOCOLATE PRETZELS

SWEET MICE

Round wooden picks
1 (13-ounce) bag milk chocolate kisses, unwrapped
3 (2-ounce) vanilla bark coating squares, melted
3 (2-ounce) chocolate bark coating squares, melted
Sliced almonds
1 (12-ounce) package licorice
1 (0.75-ounce) tube red or brown writing gel

Insert a round wooden pick in the bottom center of each kiss. Place on a wax paper-lined baking sheet, and freeze 30 minutes.

Dip half of the kisses in vanilla bark coating; place on wax paper. Immediately place almonds behind point of kiss, pressing gently to form ears. Repeat procedure with remaining kisses, chocolate bark coating, and almonds. Let dry completely.

Remove wooden picks, and insert a 2-inch piece of licorice into hole to form a tail. Make dots for eyes and nose with writing gel. Yield: 64 candies.

CHOCOLATE PRETZELS

Savor the perfect marriage of salty and sweet with chocolate-drenched pretzels. Once they're dry, stack them between layers of wax paper in an airtight container; store in a cool, dry place up to one month.

1 (10-ounce) package pretzel rods, cut in half, if desired
1 (24-ounce) package vanilla bark coating, melted
1 (24-ounce) package chocolate bark coating, melted
Garnishes: finely chopped nuts, candy sprinkles, almond brickle chips, additional melted bark coating

Dip half of pretzels in vanilla bark coating; place on wax paper to dry. Repeat procedure with remaining pretzels and chocolate bark coating. Dip pretzels again, and garnish, if desired. Yield: 2½ dozen.

CHUNKS OF SNOW

1 pound white chocolate bark coating, chopped
1 (3.5-ounce) jar macadamia nuts
1 (6-ounce) package sweetened dried cranberries

Melt coating in a saucepan over low heat, stirring constantly. Remove from heat; stir in nuts and dried cranberries. Spread mixture onto a lightly greased baking sheet. Cool. Break into pieces. Yield: 1½ pounds.

SUGAR AND SPICE GORP

Package this recipe in peanut cans wrapped in ribbon or paper and finished off with raffia or twine bows. You'll need an extra 12-ounce can for packaging this recipe. Save the extra peanuts in a zip-top bag for snacking.

1 egg white
1 tablespoon butter or margarine, melted
1 (12-ounce) can cocktail peanuts
1⅓ cups sugar
1 tablespoon plus 1 teaspoon ground cinnamon
2 teaspoons ground nutmeg
1 teaspoon ground allspice
½ cup raisins
½ cup coarsely chopped dried apricots
1 cup candy-coated chocolate pieces

Beat egg white at high speed with an electric mixer until stiff peaks form; stir in butter. Add peanuts, tossing to coat.

Combine sugar and next 3 ingredients in a large zip-top plastic bag. Add ¼ cup butter-coated peanuts to sugar mixture, tossing to coat. Remove sugar-coated peanuts with a slotted spoon to a baking sheet coated with cooking spray. Repeat procedure with remaining sugar mixture and butter-coated peanuts.

Bake at 300° for 20 minutes, stirring after 10 minutes. Let cool.

Combine sugar-coated peanuts, raisins, and remaining ingredients; stir well. Yield: 5 cups.

PEPPER NUTS

2 (6-ounce) cans whole natural almonds
3 tablespoons butter or margarine
3 tablespoons white wine Worcestershire sauce
1 teaspoon salt
1 teaspoon chili powder
½ teaspoon garlic powder
⅛ teaspoon ground white pepper
⅛ teaspoon ground red pepper
⅛ teaspoon black pepper

Place almonds in a medium bowl. Melt butter in a small skillet or saucepan. Stir in Worcestershire sauce and remaining 6 ingredients. Cook 1 minute. Remove from heat, and pour over almonds; stir well. Let stand 30 minutes.

Arrange almonds in a single layer on an ungreased jellyroll pan or baking sheet. Bake at 300° for 35 minutes, stirring often. Cool completely. Yield: 2 cups.

COFFEE CAKE CROUTONS

The taste of this easy dessert brings to mind a freshly baked coffee cake. It makes a great late-night snack or breakfast treat.

1   (10¾-ounce) frozen pound cake, thawed
⅔   cup sugar
⅓   cup strong brewed coffee
¼   cup Kahlúa or other coffee liqueur
1   cup toasted pecans, ground
¼   cup sugar

Trim crust from pound cake, and cut cake into 1-inch cubes. Combine ⅔ cup sugar and coffee in a small saucepan; bring to a boil over medium heat, stirring often. Boil 1 minute. Remove from heat; cool 1 minute. Stir in liqueur. Pour coffee syrup mixture into a small bowl, and let cool completely.

Combine pecans and ¼ cup sugar; stir well. Working quickly, dip each cake cube into coffee syrup. Roll each cube in pecan mixture, coating completely. Let cake cubes dry at room temperature on wire racks at least 2 hours. Yield: 3 dozen.

COFFEE CAKE CROUTONS

ESPRESSO FUDGE

Espresso granules have abundant flavor that mellows with hazelnuts and chocolate cookie crumbs. This recipe is so rich you'll want to cut it into tiny squares.

15   chocolate wafer cookies
¼   cup instant espresso granules, divided
1½   cups sugar
½   cup butter or margarine
1   (5-ounce) can evaporated milk
8   ounces vanilla bark coating, chopped
1   (7-ounce) jar marshmallow cream
½   cup chopped hazelnuts
1   teaspoon vanilla extract

Position knife blade in food processor bowl. Add cookies and 2 tablespoons espresso granules; process until mixture resembles fine crumbs. Set aside.

Line a 13- x 9-inch pan with a large sheet of aluminum foil, allowing foil to extend 1 inch beyond ends of pan. Butter the foil, and set aside.

Combine remaining 2 tablespoons espresso granules, sugar, ½ cup butter, and milk in a large saucepan. Cook over low heat until sugar and espresso granules dissolve, stirring occasionally. Bring to a boil over medium heat, stirring constantly. Boil 5 minutes, stirring constantly, until mixture reaches soft ball stage or a candy thermometer registers 234°. Remove from heat.

Add candy coating and marshmallow cream, stirring until candy coating melts. Stir in hazelnuts and vanilla. Gently fold in reserved cookie crumb mixture, creating a speckled effect.

Spread mixture into prepared pan. Let cool completely. Carefully lift foil out of pan. Cut fudge into small squares. Yield: 2 pounds.

ESPRESSO FUDGE

CUMBERLAND SAUCE

This sweet-yet-tart sauce is terrific with pork and turkey, or even as a glaze for ham.

2½ cups port wine, divided
 1 (10½-ounce) jar red currant jelly
 3 tablespoons light brown sugar
 2 tablespoons grated orange rind
 ⅔ cup orange juice
1½ tablespoons grated fresh ginger
 2 teaspoons dry mustard
 ¼ teaspoon salt
 ¼ teaspoon ground red pepper
2½ tablespoons cornstarch

Bring 2 cups wine, jelly, and next 7 ingredients to a boil in a large saucepan, stirring constantly; reduce heat, and simmer, stirring often, 20 minutes.

Stir together remaining ½ cup wine and cornstarch until smooth. Stir into hot mixture; bring to a boil over medium heat. Boil, stirring constantly, 1 minute; cool. Pour sauce into sterilized jars, seal, and store in refrigerator up to 1 month. Yield: about 4 cups.

APPLESAUCE

Choose decorative jars for packaging this old-fashioned favorite. Complete the festive look with homemade labels tied on with twine or ribbon.

12 large Granny Smith apples, peeled and coarsely chopped
1½ cups sugar
 ¼ cup fresh lemon juice

Cook all ingredients in a Dutch oven over low heat, stirring often, 10 minutes. (Sugar will dissolve, and apples will begin to break down and release juices.) Increase to medium heat, and cook, stirring often, 25 more minutes or until thickened. Spoon into sterilized jars, seal, and store in refrigerator up to 1 month. Yield: about 6 cups.

CARAMEL SAUCE

 1 cup butter
 2 cups sugar
 2 teaspoons fresh lemon juice
1½ cups whipping cream

Melt butter in a heavy saucepan over medium heat; add sugar and lemon juice, and cook, stirring constantly, about 7 minutes or until mixture turns a light caramel color, or about 8½ minutes for a medium color, or up to about 10 minutes for a dark color. (The medium color produced the most popular flavor among our taste testers.) Gradually add cream, and cook, stirring constantly, 1 to 2 minutes or until smooth. Remove from heat, and let cool.

Pour sauce into sterilized jars, seal, and store in refrigerator up to 1 month. Yield: about 3 cups.

Note: Be very careful when adding the whipping cream to the hot caramel sauce. It creates steam, and the liquid will splatter slightly.

TIP Don't overlook safety when giving food gifts. Sterilize jars by boiling them, covered with water, for 15 minutes. Fill jars while still hot. Refrigerate sauces immediately, and be sure that your friends and relatives know to keep them cold. It's easy for a small gift to be lost in the holiday shuffle, so hand-deliver yours, and ask that it be stored in the refrigerator right away.

CARAMEL SAUCE, CUMBERLAND SAUCE, AND APPLESAUCE

ORANGES IN ORANGE LIQUEUR

ORANGES IN ORANGE LIQUEUR

The fruit will retain its bright orange appearance for months—if you can resist it that long.

- 3 to 4 oranges, unpeeled and sliced
- 1 cup sugar
- ½ cup water
- ½ cup orange liqueur

Pack orange slices into a 1-quart jar, and set aside.

Bring sugar and ½ cup water to a boil in a saucepan, stirring constantly. Boil 1 minute, and remove from heat.

Stir in liqueur, and pour over orange slices. Cover tightly, and store in refrigerator up to 2 months. Serve oranges and liqueur over pound cake or ice cream. Yield: 3½ cups.

FLEA MARKET GIFTS

Shop flea markets and estate sales for old glass bowls and other small containers to accompany homemade fruit preserves. Look for beautiful bargains such as old pressed-glass compotes or sugar bowls.

basket of wine

The customary bottle of wine takes on distinctive style when tucked in a twig basket spray-painted gold. A good time to buy baskets at great prices is just after Easter. Spray-paint baskets gold or silver for Christmas. Wire faux grape clusters (found at most discount and import stores) to the handle, and tie on a sparkling ribbon for a spirited presentation. A package of cocktail crackers along with the wine is an appropriate addition.

wine ideas

Food is always an appropriate gift. After all, everyone loves to eat. But gift food needn't be homemade to be heartfelt. During the holidays, your schedule may not include much time in the kitchen. Packaging purchased food, or wine as we did here, will ensure your reputation as a thoughtful (and creative) giver. If you're giving a hostess gift, plan ahead and ask what will be served, then choose the wine to complement the meal. Or, select a dessert wine to offer a sweet ending to the affair. And, for special friends and holiday occasions, fill a basket with a bottle of champagne.

children in the kitchen
make these fun food gifts with the kids

Looking for gifts your children can make for teachers and loved ones? Create these tasty treats with limited preparation time and pantry ingredients. Wrap Candy Cane Swizzle Sticks in cellophane, and place these flavorful stirrers in a mug for hot cocoa or coffee. Festive Candy Shop Pizza Cookies packaged in pizza boxes make fun gifts for any special grown-up.

HOLIDAY TREES, CANDY CANE SWIZZLE STICKS, AND MINIATURE PEANUT BUTTER CRACKER BITES

HOLIDAY TREES

Your kids will unleash their imaginations when decorating these goodies.

    Green food coloring paste
  8 (2-ounce) white chocolate bark
     coating squares, chopped and
     melted
 12 pointed ice-cream cones
    Toppings: green and white sparkling
     sugars, holiday sprinkles, candy-
     coated chocolate pieces, gumdrops

Stir paste into melted candy coating until blended and desired color is achieved. Dip each cone into coating; immediately sprinkle with green sugar. Press candies into coating; press 1 gumdrop on the top of each cone. Dry on a wire rack. Pour white sparkling sugar into a clear plastic cup, and add tree; place in a plastic bag, and tie with ribbon, if desired. Yield: 12 trees.

CANDY CANE SWIZZLE STICKS

  4 (2-ounce) vanilla bark coating
     squares, chopped and melted
    Green food coloring paste
 12 large candy canes
    Toppings: colored sprinkles and
     sugars

Stir together melted candy coating and desired amount of paste. (We used a wooden pick dipped once in paste to tint coating.) Dip ends of candy canes 2 to 3 inches into coating; let excess drip off. Sprinkle immediately with desired toppings, and dry on a wire rack. Yield: 12 candy canes.

CANDY SHOP PIZZA COOKIES

CANDY SHOP PIZZA COOKIES

Decorate pizza boxes with green spray paint to deliver these homespun gifts.

- 10 tablespoons butter or margarine, softened
- ½ cup sugar
- ½ cup firmly packed light brown sugar
- 1 tablespoon dark brown sugar
- 1 large egg
- ½ teaspoon vanilla extract
- 1½ cups all-purpose flour
- ½ teaspoon baking soda
- ½ teaspoon salt
- 1 cup (6 ounces) semisweet chocolate morsels, divided
- 1 cup (6 ounces) white chocolate morsels, divided
- ½ cup chunky peanut butter
- Toppings: holiday sprinkles, candy-coated chocolate pieces, white chocolate pretzels
- White chocolate, melted

Beat first 4 ingredients at medium speed with an electric mixer until creamy. Add egg and vanilla; blend well.

Combine flour, soda, and salt; gradually add to butter mixture, beating well after each addition. Stir in ½ cup each of semisweet and white chocolate morsels. Spread dough evenly onto 2 lightly greased 6-inch round pizza pans.

Bake at 375° for 20 to 25 minutes or until lightly browned. Working quickly, sprinkle crust with remaining semisweet and white chocolate morsels; drop peanut butter by tablespoonfuls onto crust. Let stand 5 minutes or until morsels and peanut butter are softened; gently spread evenly over crust. Decorate with desired toppings; drizzle pizza with melted white chocolate. Yield: 2 (6-inch) pizzas.

Note: Substitute 1 lightly greased 12-inch pizza pan for 2 (6-inch) pans, if desired.

MINIATURE PEANUT BUTTER CRACKER BITES

Your kids will love the classic flavor combination of these peanut butter and chocolate treats. Try and save some to give away as gifts!

- 3 (2-ounce) chocolate bark coating squares
- 1 tablespoon shortening
- 3 dozen miniature round peanut butter-filled crackers

Combine candy coating and shortening in the top of a double boiler. Bring water to a boil in double boiler; reduce heat, and simmer. Place chocolate and shortening over water, and cook, stirring constantly, until melted.

Dip crackers in chocolate, and place on wax paper. Chill 15 minutes or until chocolate hardens. Yield: 3 dozen.

COLA CANDY

- 3½ cups vanilla wafer crumbs
- 2 cups powdered sugar
- 1 cup chopped pecans
- ½ cup cola soft drink
- 2 tablespoons butter or margarine, melted
- Cola Frosting

Stir together first 5 ingredients; shape mixture into 1-inch balls. Cover and chill at least 30 minutes.

Dip balls in Cola Frosting; chill until ready to serve. Yield: 2 dozen.

cola frosting:

- ¾ cup powdered sugar
- ¼ teaspoon vanilla extract
- ¼ cup butter or margarine, softened
- ⅓ cup cola soft drink

Stir together all ingredients. Yield: 1½ cups.

wrappings & tags

wired stars

Bring a stellar dimension to your gifts with metallic stars. Take two star
stickers, put a thin wire between them, and press together. Attach the
other end of the wire to the ribbon wrapped around the present. For
variety, use different sizes and colors of stickers.

paper gift pouches

Punch holes in two squares of decorative paper, weave ribbon through the holes, fill the pouch with a tiny gift, and tie the ribbon in a bow for a beautiful little package. Stamp an initial or other design on the front, if desired, to embellish the wrapping.

a cheery theme

Enhance the impact of your wrappings by using materials in one main color (left). Small boxes wrapped in shades of red and tied with complementary red-checked ribbons are delightful to behold. Decorate paper tags with buttons, rickrack, and old Christmas stamps for a totally coordinated ensemble.

add little extras

For a soft sheen, wrap a tissue-covered box with waxed or glassine (semi-transparent) paper (above). Layer elements to plump up the bow such as the miniature winter scarf and candy cane pictured here. For the coordinating gift tag, create an instant winter scene with snowflake stickers and three little buttons glued to a square of paper.

tagged for fun

Tie on the charm with creative gift cards that are easy to make yet add distinctive flair (below). A monochromatic color scheme is an attractive backdrop for this whimsical gift tag. To make the card, fold a piece of card stock paper in half. Glue a rectangle of printed paper on the front of the card. Glue shaped buttons and charms onto the printed paper cutout. Punch a hole in the corner, and tie to the bow with a thin cord or thread.

woodsy trims

Accent your Christmas boxes with decorative acorns, berries, and raffia for striking good looks. Permanent woodland ornaments are shown, but nuts and berries from your backyard will work, as well. For wrapping several gifts into one, make a tower of different sized boxes and secure them with a wide ribbon, tying a bow at the top.

mitten tags

Mitten gift tags make this the cutest package under the tree, hands down. Trace the mitten pattern on page 248 onto tracing paper, and transfer the shape onto thin colored craft foam sheets or card stock. Cut out the tag, and embellish it with a paint pen. Add festivity and flamboyance to the package with jingle bells and ribbons.

fruitful package toppers

A combination of fruit, ribbon, and beads creates handsome decorations for special gifts.

For the fruit embellishments, cut fruit from the main stem of a fruit pick, leaving a bit of the stem intact. Tie the stem into the knot of the bow.

For fruit clusters, tape the stems of several different fruits together, and tie them into the bow. To attach other fruits, such as apples and pears, simply glue each piece to the package as desired. To add beads, attach them to a string or a stem, tape them together to form a cluster, and tie them into the bow. For the most secure arrangement, knot the ribbon over the stems, and tie a bow over the knot. Look for materials at crafts, discount, and import stores.

gifts by mail
package your gifts for safe travel

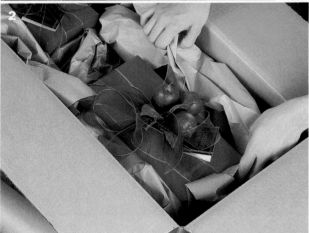

Now that they're wrapped to perfection, make sure your packages stay that way. Follow these suggestions to ensure that your gifts arrive at their destinations in perfect condition.

1 Wrap your packages and have them ready to mail three to four weeks before Christmas (even earlier if you're sending them overseas). Select a cardboard box in good condition that is large enough to allow for adequate cushioning materials on all sides of your gift.

2 Pad the bottom of the box with several inches of packing material. Choose the packing material that will cushion your gift the best—such as brown paper or newspaper, shredded paper, or bubble wrap. Using several types of cushioning, such as bubble wrap and shredded paper, is most effective. Use enough packing material that the contents of the box do not move when you shake it. Before sealing, place a duplicate address label on the inside of the box.

3 Seal your box with a strong two-inch-wide tape that is reinforced, pressure-sensitive, or water-activated. Do not use cellophane tape, masking tape, string, or twine. Place one clearly written address label on the top of the box, but not on a seam or on the sealing tape. Include a complete return address in the top left-hand corner of your label.

MORE TIPS

• Place the gift in the center of the box and stuff additional packing material firmly around all sides.
• Make sure boxes with breakables are clearly labeled "Fragile," so that shippers will know to handle them with care.
• When shipping food, label the box "Perishables," so that the recipient will know that the box should be opened right away.

stamped sacks

Use a rubber stamp to decorate these easy no-sew gift bags that will make gift wrapping a pleasure (above).

To begin, cut a piece of burlap to the desired size. Use a foam paintbrush and fabric paints to paint the entire design of a rubber stamp. Press the stamp to the fabric using enough pressure to transfer the image. Continue stamping to achieve the desired design. Clean the stamp before stamping with different colors. (To clean the stamp, spray it with household cleaner and let it sit for a couple of minutes; wash away remaining paint with warm water.) After stamping the design, allow the paint to dry before making the bag.

To make the bag, fold the stamped fabric in half, with wrong sides facing and edges aligned. Turn one side edge under ¼ inch and overlap the other side edge. Glue the side edges together. Let dry. Turn the bottom edge under ¼ inch, and overlap the other bottom edge. Glue the bottom edges together. Let dry. Ravel the top edge, and tie with a bow. For a matching tag, stamp a design on a square of paper.

initial wraps

Create your own gift wrap designs by stamping kraft paper with an initial stamp—either your own initial or the gift recipient's (left). Either way, it's a unique way to embellish plain paper. We colored the design with a felt tip pen.

clearly pretty

For a quick, elegant-looking presentation, place a small gift in a tissue-lined cellophane bag (below). Tie a large, ornate bead into the bow of a wide ribbon. Old chandelier pendants or pieces of costume jewelry found at flea markets or tag sales are just right for this packaging idea.

canned goods

Recycle potato chip cans for upscale containers. Wash and dry an empty potato chip can. Cut a piece of fabric large enough to wrap the entire can, allowing enough fabric to fold over the top of the can. Turn under the raw edge of the fabric at the seam, and glue the fabric in place along the seam and on the inside of the can at the top. Glue ribbon or fabric trim along the bottom of the can to hide the raw edge of the fabric.

For the top, spray-paint the plastic top gold. Let dry. Punch a hole in the center of the top and thread cording or tassels through the hole, knotting the cording on the back side of the lid to hold it in place. This is an excellent holder for candles or cookies.

little bundles

Use a variety of fabrics such as silk, flannel, or classic cotton to clothe gifts in high fashion. Cut a circle of fabric large enough to accommodate the gift. (The bags pictured are made from a 20-inch circle and use approximately ½ yard of fabric for two bags.) Trim the raw fabric edges with pinking shears.

To form a casing, with wrong sides facing, turn under one inch around the edges and machine-stitch. Use a pair of scissors to make a small slit in the casing, and thread ribbon or cording through the casing, knotting the ends. Pull both ends of the ribbon to gather the top of the gift bag, and tie in a bow to close. To trim the bags, tuck silk flowers, cinnamon sticks, or greenery into the openings.

great bows
easy steps to beautiful bows

Be a bow-tying expert with "see-and-do" directions for two pretty bow designs. In addition to showing you how to make the bows, we also give tips on making your bows exactly the size you need.

cluster bow
materials
4½ yards (1½-inch-wide) double-faced ribbon • masking tape (optional) • needle • thread to match ribbon

1 The materials listed will make a 10-inch-wide bow. To estimate ribbon yardage for a different size: multiply the diameter of the size bow you want by the number of loops you want—about eight loops for a small bow, fourteen for a medium one, and twenty for a large one. For yardage requirements, divide that total by thirty-six.

Fold the ribbon into 10-inch-wide loops arranged side by side (photo 1), leaving tails at the beginning and end. Stabilize the outside edges of the loops with masking tape, if desired.

2 Thread the needle, and knot the thread. Run several large gathering stitches through the center of each loop. Remove the tape. Pull the thread to gather the loops, making a bow (photo 2). Wrap the thread around the center of the bow, and knot it to secure.

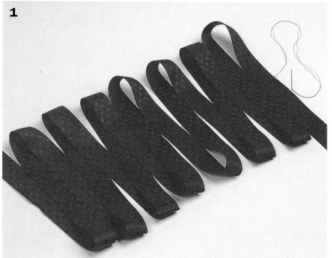

1

2

flower bow

materials

1 yard (1 ½-inch-wide) velvet ribbon • ½ yard (1 ½-inch-wide) wire-edge ribbon • florist wire • 3 jingle bells

1 The materials listed will make a 6-inch-wide bow. To make the bow smaller or larger, just cut the ribbons shorter or longer.

For the petals, cut velvet ribbon into six (6-inch) lengths. For the leaves, cut wire-edge ribbon into three (6-inch) lengths. Trim the ends to form points. Cut the wire into three (3-inch) lengths and one (5-inch) length.

2 Using the 3-inch wires, wire petals and leaves together (photo 2). Stack two petal sections on top of the leaves. String bells onto the 5-inch wire. Centering the bells on the petals, secure all three sections with the bell wire, twisting the wire ends together at the back (photo 3).

MORE TIPS Wire-edge ribbon is easy to work with, but good stiff ribbon will work, too. If you want longer streamers or lengths to wrap around the box, buy one to two extra yards.

1

2

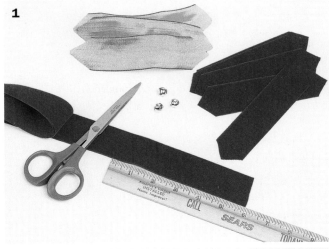

3

patterns

garden-inspired ornaments
Instructions are on page 75. Patterns are full size.

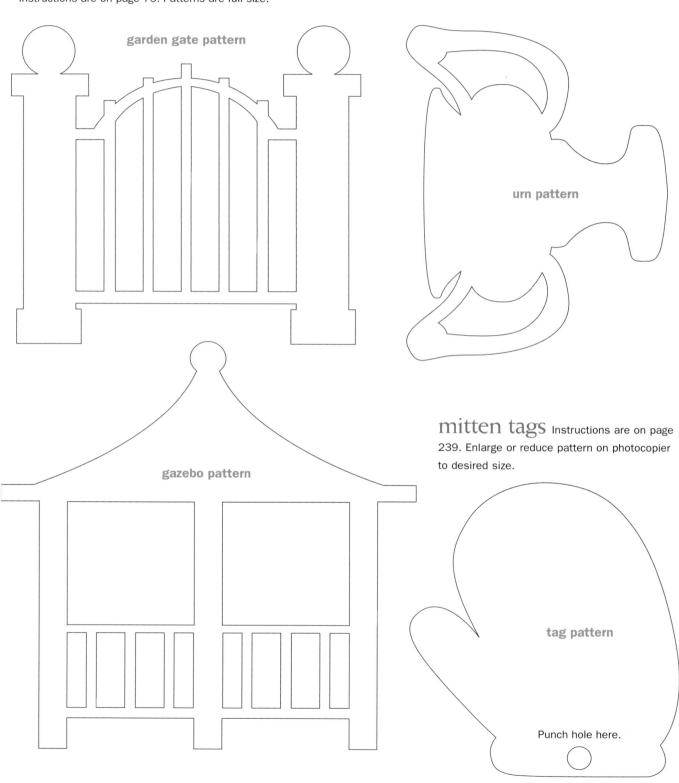

garden gate pattern

urn pattern

gazebo pattern

mitten tags Instructions are on page 239. Enlarge or reduce pattern on photocopier to desired size.

tag pattern

Punch hole here.

cut & glue decorations

Instructions are on page 93. Patterns are full size.

To cut a tree skirt from uncut felt, fold felt in half, then in half again. To mark outer circle, tie pushpin to end of 36-inch-long string. Stick pushpin through corner of felt where folds meet. Make a mark 27 inches from pushpin. Tie loose end of string to chalk at this mark. With string taut, draw arc with 27-inch radius. To mark inner circle, draw arc with 3-inch radius in same manner. Cut along marked lines through all layers; open skirt. Cut straight line from outer edge to inner circle for skirt opening.

tree skirt cutting diagram

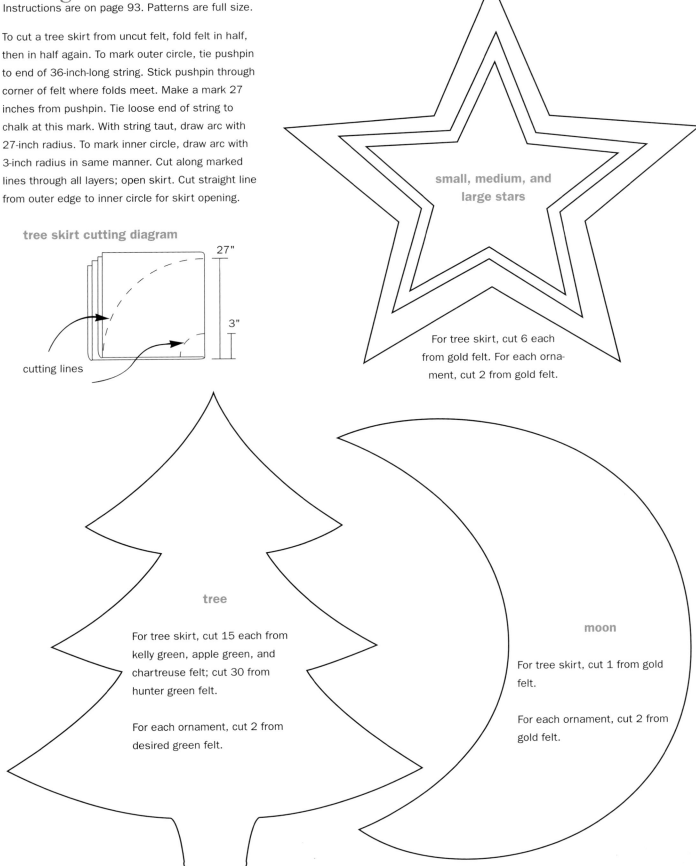

27"

3"

cutting lines

small, medium, and large stars

For tree skirt, cut 6 each from gold felt. For each ornament, cut 2 from gold felt.

tree

For tree skirt, cut 15 each from kelly green, apple green, and chartreuse felt; cut 30 from hunter green felt.

For each ornament, cut 2 from desired green felt.

moon

For tree skirt, cut 1 from gold felt.

For each ornament, cut 2 from gold felt.

index

recipe index